CONTENTS

INTRODUCTION

In January 1649, the unthinkable happened: after a public trial the King of England was beheaded on a scaffold outside his palace of Whitehall. The world would never be quite the same again. Very shortly afterwards the monarchy, along with the House of Lords, were formally abolished. England was declared to be a 'free Commonwealth' and for the next eleven years various governments attempted to forge a new concept of England based upon the ideals of Puritan republicanism and impose these ideals on Scotland, Wales and Ireland in an attempt to create not just an English but a 'British' republic.

How had this extraordinary state of affairs come about? Why had the relationship between king and Parliament broken down to such an extent that by 1642 both sides were actively preparing for war? It would be very easy to fill a large library with books and articles on the subject of the English Civil War, to say nothing of the ever-growing number of websites, films and documentaries. While this shows how popular the subject is, it can be rather overwhelming: where does one begin? That is where *The English Civil War in 100 Facts* makes its entrance! Here I have tried to set out the main story, present the major characters and introduce some of the principal issues that people fought over – many of which are still being debated.

Naturally, in a book of this length, it is impossible to explore every detail on every subject concerning this intriguing and complex period. If you are seeking detailed analysis of, say, military equipment and strategy, I am afraid you will be disappointed. I have tried to concentrate on why the people of the British Isles fought each other so bitterly and for so long, why fathers fought sons and brother killed brother, and some of the consequences that arose out of this conflict. I hope, when you read and hopefully enjoy this short book, it may prompt you to explore this fascinating period in greater depth.

1. Charles I Was Not Born to Be King

Charles, the second son of James VI of Scotland and his wife, a Danish Princess called Anne, was born in Dunfermline Palace, Fife, on 19 November 1600. Just before Christmas, Charles was baptised in Edinburgh by David Lindsey, Bishop of Ross. Charles was a small and delicate child and may have suffered from rickets. When James succeeded Elizabeth I to become King of England as well as Scotland in March 1603, Charles, considered too weak to travel, was left behind in Edinburgh under the guardianship of the Lord Fyvie.

Charles was three and a half when it was decided that he was strong enough to join the rest of the royal family in London. His governess in London was Lady Elizabeth Carey, who had strong leather boots reinforced with brass made for the young Charles in an attempt to strengthen his legs and ankles. Charles adored and idealised his elder brother, Prince Henry, who had been born in 1594, and tried hard to keep up with him. But Henry was tall and strong and teased his little, bookish brother, saying that when he became king he would make Charles his Archbishop of Canterbury. As the spare, Charles was very much in the shadow of his glamorous brother, but in November 1612 all this changed. Whether as a result of typhoid or porphyria, Henry died and little Charles was now the heir to the throne.

There is a story that young Charles once, on a progress with his father, visited the home of Sir Henry Cromwell near Huntingdon. Also present was Sir Oliver's young nephew, also called Oliver. The story goes that the two boys, Charles and Oliver, went out into the garden to play; there they quarrelled and fought, with Oliver beating Charles. One suspects that this story was invented much later: after Charles and Oliver had met and fought on the battlefield, and Charles had, again, been beaten. It is also unlikely, in a society ruled by respect for hierarchy, status and convention, that a prince of the blood would have been allowed to play with a common boy like the young Oliver.

2. Oliver Cromwell Spent One Year as an Undergraduate at Sidney Sussex, Cambridge

When not, allegedly, punching royal princes in his uncle's back garden, young Cromwell was attending Huntingdon Grammar School. There he would have learnt Latin, studied the classical authors and the Bible, attended church and made copious notes of the sermons, all under the guidance of his schoolmaster, Thomas Beard. Beard was a moderate Puritan who was not only the schoolmaster but also the vicar of All Saints' Church and, from 1611, the Church of St John the Baptist – both in Huntingdon. There has been much speculation as to the extent to which Beard's Puritanism influenced the young Cromwell. It is now impossible to say, although in 1630–31 Beard clashed with Cromwell over local political issues in Huntingdon, which suggests that their relationship was not particularly close.

In 1616, Cromwell went up to Sidney Sussex College in Cambridge. Sidney Sussex was a relatively new foundation, having been founded posthumously by Lady Frances Sidney, dowager Countess of Sussex, in 1594. Like the other Cambridge colleges founded during Elizabeth's reign (such as Emmanuel), Sidney Sussex had a reputation as a Puritan college, which may have been a factor in the Cromwell's decision to send their son there. As it turned out, Cromwell only spent one year at Sidney Sussex because in 1617 his father died and, as the only son, he inherited lands and a farm that required his presence and he also had to care for his widowed mother and seven unmarried sisters.

3. CROMWELL EXPERIENCED A PROFOUND RELIGIOUS CONVERSION IN THE LATE 1620s

In August 1620 Cromwell married Elizabeth Bourchier (1595–1665), the daughter of a wealthy London merchant. The marriage was to be important subsequently as Elizabeth's family was connected with a network of wealthy Puritan families, many of whom were to become prominent opponents of Charles I in the 1630s. But for Cromwell the 1620s were a difficult time: his income was declining, and by the end of the decade Cromwell was suffering both physically and mentally. He took the waters at Wellingborough in an attempt to ease recurring stomach cramps and in September 1628 consulted a London doctor, Sir Theodore Turquet de Mayerne, for help with what was then called *valde melancolicus* – what we would now call depression. According to later accounts by Cromwell, it was after this period of illness and depression that he experienced a religious conversion, which convinced him that he was now justified before God.

For the Puritan, the conversion experience was of profound importance and often followed a similar pattern: first came a time of doubt and uncertainty regarding one's salvation, this often being accompanied by symptoms of depression and anxiety. One would pray, search the scriptures and consult with 'godly' neighbours and ministers who would offer spiritual counselling. At some point there would be a 'road to Damascus' experience of revelation. That revelation of God's grace would be achieved when one discovered, in the depths of one's soul, the peace and joy that flows from the certainty of one's election to eternal life.

As he described it much later in a letter to his cousin, Mrs St John, Cromwell apparently experienced a textbook conversion, recounting that 'one beam [of light] in a dark place hath exceeding much refreshment in it, blessed is His name for shining upon so dark a heart as mine'. It is possible that Cromwell refashioned the account of his conversion to conform to accepted understanding of the process; nevertheless, that experience was to be of central importance in Cromwell's life. His trust in God and his conviction that he was performing God's will gave him the psychological and emotional strength and authority to go to war against Charles I in 1642, to see that war through to a successful conclusion, and, eventually, to become the most powerful man in the kingdom.

4. PURITANS LIKED LONG SERMONS

Ever since the break with Rome in the 1530s the English Church had been torn between conservatives and reformers. Conservatives, while rejecting the authority of the Pope and many Roman Catholic doctrines and practices, nevertheless wished to retain some features and ceremonies from the pre-Reformation period and insisted upon a strict uniformity of discipline and belief. The reformers, inspired by Protestant theologians on the Continent such as Zwingli and John Calvin, wanted to push the English Church in a much more radically Protestant direction, both in theology and practice. In particular they wanted to strip out any beliefs, practices or ceremonies associated with the Roman Catholic Church.

During the reign of Edward VI (1547–53), a much more radical form of Protestantism had prevailed in the Church of England than under his father Henry VIII, which was reflected in the two prayer books written by Thomas Cranmer, the Archbishop of Canterbury, in 1549 and 1552. Edward was succeeded by his half-sister, Mary, who was a Roman Catholic and determined to restore her faith in England. As part of this attempt, nearly 300 Protestants were burnt at the stake and many hundreds more fled abroad. While on the Continent these exiles came into contact with 'advanced' Protestant thinkers and theologians, particularly those associated with Calvin's theocracy in Geneva. With the accession of Elizabeth I in 1558 many Protestant exiles returned, enthused by the radical Protestantism they had experienced in Europe and determined to 'purify' the English Church and remodel it along continental lines. By the 1560s, these men and women were being derisively called 'Puritans' or 'Precisians.'

During Elizabeth's reign there was an uneasy balance maintained between conservatives and reformers – or Anglicans and Puritans, as we might call them. The Queen herself disliked Puritanism, believing its tenets and attitudes weakened royal authority and social discipline, a view shared by her successor, James VI and I. As we shall see, periodic attempts by Puritans to challenge the religious settlement of 1559 caused headaches for both Elizabeth and her bishops, many of whom sympathised with aspects of the reformers' agenda.

The Queen also had more personal reasons to dislike the Puritans, having been deeply offended by a book published in 1558 by the Scottish Puritan John Knox. Knox was a follower of John Calvin and was to become one of the leaders of the Reformation in Scotland. He wrote a book from Geneva called *The First Blast of the Trumpet Against the Monstrous Regiment of Women*, in which he denounced female rulers as contrary to God's law. His specific targets were two Catholic female rulers, Mary of England and Mary of Guise, Dowager Queen of Scotland and regent for her daughter, Mary. But from his specific attack on Catholic female rulers, Knox then went on to denounce any female ruler, stating that 'God, by the order of his creation, has [deprived] women of authority and dominion'. He went on:

> For who can deny but it repugneth to nature, that the blind shall be appointed to lead and conduct such as do see? That the weak, the sick, and impotent persons shall nourish and keep the whole and strong, and finally, that the foolish, mad and fanatic shall govern the discrete, and give counsel to such as be sober of mind? And such be all women, compared unto man in bearing of authority. For their sight in civil regiment, is but blindness: their strength, weakness: their counsel, foolishness: and judgement, fantasy, if it be rightly considered.

Elizabeth, as queen, took great exception to Knox. So much so that when he returned to Scotland in 1559 Elizabeth ordered that he should not be allowed to set foot in England, later she blocked any influence Knox may have hoped to exercise in relations between the Church of England and the Kirk of Scotland.

The strength of Puritanism was rooted in a Protestant theological conviction first articulated by Martin Luther, called 'justification by faith alone', and in reliance upon the Bible as the revealed and infallible word of God. Puritans believed that each person should read and interpret the Bible for him or herself, aided and supported by the community of the 'godly', and that the Bible alone was the final authority in matters of doctrine, worship and morality. They also believed that the Roman Catholic Church had corrupted and perverted 'true religion' over the centuries and that Roman Catholic doctrines and ceremonies were inherently wrong and dangerous. Thus Puritans rejected nearly all ceremony and imagery in the church, along with singing, chanting and vestments. Their churches and chapels were plain and functional, their services based upon the reading of the Bible and its interpretation delivered in long sermons. Thus they condemned the remnants of ritual and music left in Elizabeth's church as 'the dregs of popery'. Also, they increasingly denounced the government of bishops in the Church and argued that the Presbyterian system was nearer to the practice of the early church as revealed in the New Testament.

In its theology Puritanism became synonymous with the beliefs of John Calvin (1509–64), who preached a doctrine of election and predestination. God, according to Calvin, had preordained who would be saved and who damned since before the creation of the world. Those who, through a conversion experience, believed themselves to be saved were called 'the elect' or the 'godly'. Calvinism was very influential in the Elizabethan and Jacobean Church and the conviction of one's election often gave Calvinists a unique psychological confidence, as we saw when considering Oliver Cromwell's conversion experience.

In its social policy, Puritanism demanded a very high standard of public and private morality – the Puritan was supposed to be sober and serious. Also, as the elect were always a minority in any society, they had a duty to police the lives and morals of the mass of the un-elect, or 'the reprobate', as they were called, imposing a strict social discipline. Because Calvinism was so influential in England between 1560 and 1660, on the next page I have given you the main points organised under five headings, which together spell the acrostic TULIP.

5. The Five Points of Classical Calvinism Form the Acronym TULIP

1. Total Depravity
As a result of the Fall, man is so sunk in sin and depravity that he is unable, by his own efforts, to save himself. Left to ourselves we are all condemned to Hell.

2. Undeserved Election
God, in his mercy, reaches down and saves some individuals from the results of their depravity and sanctifies them. As God is omnipotent and omniscient, he must have known who was to be saved and who damned before the creation. Those he chooses to save are called 'the elect' and their salvation depends totally on the arbitrary choice of God and not on their innate qualities – their salvation/election is undeserved by their own merits. There was a debate among Calvinist theologians as to whether God had predestined those to election and damnation before or after the Fall (prelapsarianism or supralapsarianism).

3. Limited Atonement
Christ's death on the cross was not for all mankind, but only for the elect.

4. Irresistible Grace
The saving action of God in choosing the elect is irresistible, the elect have no choice but to be saved and their salvation does not depend in any way on their will to be saved. The damned may will to be saved, but without the saving grace of God they will still be damned.

5. Perseverance of the Saint

Once aware of one's election, through the action of God's grace vouchsafed to the individual through a conversion experience, the saints can never fall from grace.

This point was also debated by Calvinist theologians, some arguing that it led to antinomianism – the belief that one could act in any way one wished as one was saved for all eternity. Other theologians argued that an outward sign of one's election was to live a godly life and that licentiousness was a sign that one's claim to election was false.

6. Puritans Believed They Should Stop Others Enjoying Themselves

We noted earlier the Puritan belief that they had a duty to police their societies, impose strict social discipline and actively pursue 'Godly reformation'. In practice this meant supervising as closely as possible the behaviour and morals, both private and public, of their communities and parishes; condemning, punishing and abolishing all behaviour and customs that contravened the Puritan vision of godliness. This could include anything from the destruction of images, altars and stained-glass windows in churches to the closure of unlicensed 'tippling houses', the cutting down of maypoles, the public humiliation of men and women who behaved 'lewdly', the banning of church ales, the closure of theatres, and, most famously, the abolition of Christmas.

That such attacks upon the traditional pleasures and pastimes of ordinary people were unpopular is something of an understatement. The self-righteous interference into other people's lives, along with high taxation and general war-weariness, did more than anything else to alienate people from the Parliamentary cause in the late 1640s. At Christmas 1647 there was serious rioting in Canterbury and Ipswich when the authorities sought to stop Christmas festivities. Ultimately the 'godly' were not numerous or powerful enough to reform their neighbours by force.

7. Puritans Believed In the Need for Spiritual Warfare

One point upon which most Puritans were agreed was that the Christian life was one of continual struggle against the Devil and his agents in the world. Their reading of the Bible, particularly the Old Testament, convinced them that the world was a battleground between the forces of light and darkness, with themselves as the agents of light. For many Puritans this belief in the need for spiritual warfare included a corresponding belief that the end of the world was near and 'King Jesus' would soon return to earth and reign through his elect.

We can see something of the implications of the need for spiritual warfare in the activities of William Dowsing (1596–1668.) Dowsing was a Suffolk Puritan and a staunch supporter of Parliament. In December 1643, he was appointed by the Earl of Manchester as 'Commissioner for removing the Monuments of Idolatry and Superstition from the Churches of Cambridgeshire and Suffolk'. Over the next year Dowsing went around these counties smashing stained-glass windows, smashing statues, fonts, altars and altar rails, destroying or whitewashing over paintings, tearing up vestments and copies of the *Book of Common Prayer* in a systematic campaign to cleanse the churches of 'the rags of popery'. Dowsing kept a detailed diary of his activities, recording in detail both what he destroyed and what he ordered churchwardens to destroy. Sometimes, as at Pembroke College, Cambridge, he faced opposition; on this occasion it was from the Fellows, who argued that what he was doing was not only sacrilege but also illegal. Resistance usually took on a more passive form, such as the churchwarden who claimed that he did not have a ladder long enough to reach and smash the high windows in his church.

8. James VI and I Favoured the Arminians

We have seen that after the Reformation the Church of England was divided between conservatives and reformers. By the late sixteenth century this division was increasingly expressed by differing attitudes to the Calvinist doctrines of election and predestination. A Dutch theologian Jakob Hermanszoon, known by the Latinised version of his name as Jacobus Arminius (1560–1609), had protested against the rigour and determinism of the full Calvinist doctrine. Arminius argued that a god of love would not condemn the majority of mankind to everlasting torment in Hell, and that the determinist nature of Calvinism – there was nothing you could do to influence your election or damnation – robbed man of his freedom and sense of responsibility to work out his own salvation for himself.

Many saw Arminius as a Protestant heretic, but many others were attracted to the idea that salvation was not preordained, that God wished all to be saved, and that the individual could – with the help of the Church, the sacraments, prayer, reflection etc. – seek to know and do God's will and hope in eternal life. This liberal doctrine became known as Arminianism. In England, Arminian ideas began to be published and debated in the last decade of Elizabeth's reign and when James VI of Scotland became simultaneously James I of England in 1603 he discovered in the Arminian clergy a group of theologians much more to his taste than the rather forbidding Calvinist Presbyterians who dominated the Scottish Kirk.

James was thirteen months old when he became King of Scots in 1567 and as he grew to majority he came to resent the way the Kirk dominated the Crown. His Presbyterian tutors taught him in no uncertain terms that the king was subordinate to the Kirk and only ruled with the permission of the Kirk. One of the reasons James came to believe so firmly in the divine right of kings was in reaction to what he saw as the arrogance of the Kirk. Kings, James wrote, are appointed by God and are answerable to no earthly power but to God alone. They are supreme in their kingdoms and all subjects, whether lay or clerical, high or low, owe a duty of obedience and non-resistance to the Crown. Fortunately for James, the English Arminians were more than happy to exult royal authority and preach on divine right and the duty of obedience. They were also happy to echo the views of both Elizabeth and James that Puritanism was socially divisive and would, unless checked, challenge royal authority both in church and state.

Throughout his reign James promoted Arminians to high office in the church and in the universities of Oxford and Cambridge. A contemporary joke has one man asking another, 'What to the Arminians hold?' In other words, what are their beliefs? The answer given is 'All the best jobs in the Church!' The advancement of Arminians was viewed with horror by the 'godly' who saw them as crypto-papists. Their concern was increased when the Arminians embarked on a campaign to restore what was called 'the beauty of holiness' in English churches and cathedrals. They wished to restore and beautify the churches, bringing back many traditional features of Christian life and practice that had either fallen out of use in the previous hundred years, or had been attacked as 'popish'. They were also keen to encourage respect for the Church's ritual year and to ensure that the liturgy was performed with reverence and decency. In the 1620s and 1630s, this campaign to transform the appearance and practice of the English Church was to centre on intense controversy over the placing of the communion table within the church.

9. THE ENGLISH CIVIL WAR WAS FOUGHT OVER A PIECE OF FURNITURE

We have just seen how, under James VI and I, Arminians were promoted within the Church; this process accelerated when Charles became king in 1625. Charles was a convinced Arminian, he accepted his father's teachings on the divine right of kings without question and viewed Puritans as subversive; he also loved the colour, order and ritual restored to the church. In 1628, Charles appointed William Laud (1573–1645) as Bishop of London and then, in 1633, Archbishop of Canterbury. Laud was a man in a hurry; he sought to impose his vision of Arminian orthodoxy on the English Church. He ordered that the communion table in all churches and cathedrals should be returned to the eastern end of the church in the chancel, that the table should be turned north–south against the east wall, that it should be railed in to protect it from profane usage and that, if possible, the table should be raised on steps.

These orders were a radical departure from the vision of Thomas Cranmer set forth in his prayer books of 1549 and 1552. Instead of the Catholic altar set against the east wall where Mass was celebrated, Cranmer envisaged a wooden table, which, when Holy Communion, or the Lord's Supper, was to be celebrated would be carried either into the middle of the chancel or into the body of the church and set on an east–west axis. Those members of the congregation who wished to take communion would then stand, sit or kneel on three sides of the table, while the minister stood on the north side to read the liturgy. The idea was that communicants gathered around the table in the same manner as people gathered around a table for a meal.

Cranmer's vision was rarely implemented, and Elizabeth I insisted that colour, ceremony and music be retained in the services she attended in her chapel royal; the Queen's example was also followed in some of the cathedrals. Also, Holy Communion was usually only celebrated in most churches around three or four times a year and at other times the communion table tended to be pushed away into a corner and rather neglected. By Charles I's time there were complaints that the table was being used as a hatstand or that schoolboys dumped their satchels on it when entering church, it was even alleged that dogs found the legs of the table a useful place to relieve themselves. This is the background to Laud's attempt to rescue the communion table from such profane use and to restore it to what he considered its rightful place of honour within the church. At the very least, he argued, putting rails around the table would keep the dogs away! But those of a Puritan disposition saw in all this something far more sinister than just an attempt to frustrate dogs: returning the table to the eastern end, turning it altar-wise, railing it, raising it on steps, covering it with a fine linen cloth etc., all smacked of popery! They saw the Protestant communion table being transformed into a Catholic altar, and an altar was not where the reformed service of the Lord's Supper was celebrated, but the popish Mass!

Battle was joined over the position of the table and its rails. Petitions against the eastward position were read out in Parliament and sermons denounced, in ringing tones, the creeping popery being sponsored by senior Anglican clergy. In 1629 Charles dissolved Parliament, putting an end to the petitioning, but the battle resumed when Parliament finally reassembled in 1640. By then, many Puritans believed the attempt to reposition the communion table was one more step in a premeditated plan on the part of Charles and the Arminians to subvert 'the true Protestant religion' and restore Roman Catholicism in England. As the 1630s progressed, some Puritans even began to think that they might have to fight to defend England against a restoration of popery!

10. The Duke of Buckingham Was Favourite to Two Kings

George Villiers (1592–1628) has had a bad press; he has been called vain, ambitious, arrogant and incompetent. He was the favourite of James VI and I, befriended Prince Charles and remained his favourite when he became king, thus he has the rare distinction of being court favourite to two successive monarchs. Born into a minor gentry family, he entered the court aged twenty-one in 1614. Tall, handsome, intelligent and an excellent dancer, he quickly caught the eye of James, who had a liking for good-looking young men. Villiers soon replaced the then royal favourite, a Scot called Robert Carr, and James lavished gifts and honours upon him. In 1615 he was knighted, in 1616 created a viscount, then an earl in 1617, while in 1618 he was created the Marquess of Buckingham. In 1619 he was created Lord High Admiral and, finally, in 1632, a duke. Buckingham became the most powerful man at court, controlling access to the king while he, his family and his clients became very rich.

There has been much speculation whether James and Buckingham were lovers, certainly they were very close and James could hardly bear to have Buckingham out of his sight. James's nickname for Buckingham was 'Steenie', after St Stephen, who was said to have had the face of an angel. In his letters to Buckingham, James referred to him as his, 'sweet child and wife', signing himself, 'your dear father and husband'. When restoration work was carried out in the early twenty-first century on Apethorpe Palace, one of Buckingham's country houses in Northamptonshire, a secret passage was discovered linking Buckingham's bedroom to that used by James when he stayed at Apethorpe.

11. In 1623 Prince Charles and Buckingham Made a 'Secret' Visit to Spain

As part of his hopes to heal the religious divisions in Europe, James VI and I wished to marry Prince Charles to the Spanish infanta, Maria Anna. When the negotiations flagged, Charles and Buckingham hit upon a daring scheme of riding to Madrid incognito and appearing suddenly, as if out of nowhere, before the infanta and the Spanish court, there Charles would declare his love and ask her to marry him. Bowled over by the swashbuckling romanticism of Charles's reckless behaviour, the infanta would agree to the match immediately.

Charles and Buckingham left England and rode south through France under the names Thomas and John Smith, writing letters back to James as they went. In these letters James was addressed as 'Dear Dad', while in his replies James referred to Charles as 'baby Charles' and Buckingham as 'Steenie'. They arrived in Madrid in early March 1623 and to say that they took the Spaniards by surprise is something of an understatement. Even the English ambassador, John Digby, Earl of Bristol, had no idea they were on their way. Unfortunately, the infanta was not swept off her feet by these 'knights errant' and made it clear that she would never marry a heretic.

The real reason the Spanish were trying to draw out the negotiations for as long as possible was that they did not want England entering the Thirty Years War on the side of the Protestants. They entertained Charles and Buckingham sumptuously, but always prevaricated when it seemed that a definite acceptance or refusal was imminent. This game went on for six months after Charles and Buckingham arrived in Madrid, until it was clear even to them that the Spanish had no intentions of negotiating the match and, angry and humiliated, they returned home empty handed.

The Spanish match had always been unpopular in England. Memories of the ill-starred marriage between Philip II and Mary Tudor in the 1550s, years of war and the Armada under Elizabeth and the fact that Spain was the major Catholic power in Europe, made it difficult to 'sell' the idea of the match to the English people and there was much rejoicing when Charles returned without the Spanish infanta. For their part, Charles and Buckingham vented their frustration by calling loudly for war with Spain, a policy Parliament enthusiastically supported. James, old and ill, could not stand against this campaign and allowed policy to be determined by 'baby Charles' and 'Steenie'. However, English Protestants, relieved that Charles did not have a Spanish Catholic wife, were soon obliged to accept a French Catholic wife when Buckingham negotiated a match between Charles and Henrietta Maria, the fifteen-year-old sister of Louis XIII of France, as part of an Anglo-French alliance against Spain.

12. The Petition of Right

Despite having arranged a marriage with the French princess, Henrietta Maria, in 1625 Charles soon found himself at war with her brother, Louis XIII. Louis was besieging the port of La Rochelle on the Bay of Biscay, which was held by French Protestants known as Huguenots. The Huguenots appealed to Charles for help and he felt obliged to go to their aid. He appointed Buckingham as commander of the expedition and Parliament voted funds to pay for it; unfortunately, the expedition was a disaster and the English were defeated. Buckingham had already shown himself to be an incompetent commander when he had led an equally disastrous raid on the Spanish port of Cadiz in 1625. Parliament, who was expected to pay for these campaigns, denounced Buckingham and threatened to impeach him. Such an attack on the royal favourite deeply offended Charles.

Charles and Buckingham were determined to send another expedition to La Rochelle, but they were desperately short of money. Charles had already imposed what was called the 'Forced Loan' in 1626 and had imprisoned a number of gentlemen who refused to pay. Given the ill feeling caused by the Forced Loan and the incompetence of Buckingham as a commander, Parliament was in no mood to authorise further payments until the King listened to their grievances. Parliament met on 17 March 1628 and declared that no grant of monies would be voted on until they had presented their complaints to the King. As well as this, a group of opposition MPs drew up a document that set out these complaints, which became known as The Petition of Right. The petition upheld what were considered to be established rights and liberties enshrined in statutes and law and which Charles was disregarding. It appealed to

Magna Carta and laws passed under various medieval monarchs to prove that the crown could not levy taxes or forced loans, etc., without the consent of Parliament. It protested at the imprisonment of people without just cause or due process and the use of martial law to bypass the regular courts and at the billeting of soldiers and sailors on civilians without their consent. Although Charles initially rejected the petition, he had no alternative but to agree to it if he wanted any money from Parliament. He reluctantly accepted the petition on 7 June and Parliament duly voted the money. However, the MPs soon had occasion to renew their campaign of criticism of Buckingham, which provoked Charles to prorogue Parliament on 26 June.

Parliament reassembled in January 1629 and Charles hoped that one problem at least had been removed as Buckingham had been assassinated the previous August, to the delight of the country and the grief of the King. But the Commons launched into an attack on Charles's religious policies and his patronage of the Arminian party. They also condemned Charles for continuing to levy an excise tax called Tonnage and Poundage without Parliament's approval, and for imprisoning John Rolle MP for refusing to pay it. Things came to a head at the beginning of March 1629 when the opposition MPs drew up the Three Resolutions. These condemned the growth of Arminianism in the Church, called upon merchants not to pay Tonnage and Poundage and declared that anyone who did pay the tax betrayed the liberties of England.

Charles was furious and ordered the Speaker, Sir John Finch, to adjourn Parliament instantly. But as the Speaker attempted to rise from his chair and end the sitting, a number of MPs sprang forward and held him down, and other MPs locked the doors of the Commons chamber. While the Speaker struggled and royal officials hammered on the locked doors the Three Resolutions were read out and received with loud cheers from the MPs; the Commons then voted its own adjournment and the Speaker was released and the doors unlocked. The King could not ignore such open defiance and on 10 March Parliament was dissolved and nine prominent opposition MPs arrested. Parliament was not to reassemble for eleven years.

13. CHARLES I WAS A GREAT PATRON OF THE ARTS

Charles I was one of the greatest art collectors and connoisseurs to sit on the English throne, and Rubens, who combined the office of court painter and Habsburg diplomat very effectively, praised him for his knowledge and insight in artistic matters. Charles had been inspired to collect by his mother and his elder brother, whose collections he inherited and became the nucleus of his own. He had also learnt a great deal from the Duke of Buckingham, who was a patron and collector himself. On becoming king he was able to greatly expand his collection, which adorned his court. He also patronised some of the leading artists of the day: Rubens, Van Dyck, Honthorst and Mytens, to name but a few. Rubens painted the great ceiling of the Banqueting House in Whitehall, which shows the blessings of the reign of James VI and I, and his apotheosis into Heaven. Van Dyck, in a series of wonderful portraits of Charles, Henrietta Maria and leading members of the court, created the image of the court in the 1630s that has endeared down the centuries. Charles was also interested in architecture and in Inigo Jones he had the services of an architect and designer of European standing. It was Inigo Jones who had built the Whitehall Banqueting House for King James and completed the Queen's House at Greenwich for Henrietta Maria – these were the first truly classical buildings to appear in England. Jones also designed the elaborate sets and costumes for the court masques, which were a combination of dance, music and drama and which, through elaborate allusion and mythological scenes, extolled the monarchy. For Charles, the patronage of the arts was one of the duties and delights of kingship. It demonstrated that the English court was as modern and as sophisticated as any in Europe and it provided a splendid setting for the ceremonial of monarchy.

Yet for Charles there was a further dimension to his patronage of the arts. It was not a coincidence that he promoted the arts and architecture while at the same time promoting Arminian ritualism in the Church. Charles enjoyed ceremony and order, his reserved nature and speech impediment made him tongue-tied and ill at ease in company. He preferred to keep his distance from his subjects and be seen as a remote and powerful king. He also believed that order and ceremony defined the proper relationship between a king and his subjects and between the various ranks of society and was eager to promote these qualities in church and state. Charles also appreciated the order, discipline and hierarchy that was characteristic of the classical architecture of Jones. Here, again, the physical setting of monarchy – splendid, ordered, disciplined and hierarchical – reflected the order and harmony of classical architecture and reflected political convictions about his role as king and his relationship with his people.

14. Ship Money Alienated Many of Those Who Had to Pay It!

As a result of his dissolution of Parliament in 1629, Charles I had to find alternative ways to finance his government. To begin with, peace was swiftly made with France and Spain and he also instructed the lawyers to comb the archives and statutes for ancient prerogative taxes that could be revived. Many such obsolete taxes were revived, such as distraint of knighthood, which fined anyone with freehold property valued at more than £40 per annum and who had not presented themselves at the coronation to be knighted. Forest fines were levied on those whose lands had encroached on areas designated royal forest, but as the maps on which such alleged encroachments were made were hundreds of years out of date this only served to annoy those who were fined. These taxes and fines were not only very unpopular, they could not provide the long-term revenues Charles needed if he was to continue to rule without a Parliament. In 1634 Charles hit upon an idea which, he hoped, would solve all his financial problems: it was called Ship Money.

Ship Money was a prerogative tax that the Crown could levy in times of national emergency to build ships for the navy. James VI and I had levied Ship Money on the City of London in 1619 without any opposition. However, the tax was supposed to be a one-off emergency measure in a time of obvious danger. Despite war on the Continent, few in 1634 could see any obvious threat to England, to which Charles replied that it was for the monarch to decide when there was an emergency which justified the levying of Ship Money. Also, the tax had always been levied only on coastal counties but in 1635 Charles commanded that every county in England and Wales should be assessed for Ship Money. Now inland counties such as Leicestershire, Staffordshire and Worcestershire, who had never paid Ship Money in the past, were being assessed and forced to contribute. No one likes paying taxes and Charles's high-handed attitude created a great deal of opposition. When the tax was levied again in 1636 and 1637 it was feared that this prerogative tax was becoming an annual event and, as it initially brought in huge amounts of money, there was a fear that it would become a permanent tax that would make the king independent of Parliament forever. As we will see, the legality of the tax was challenged in the courts and as time went on more and more taxpayers refused to pay.

15. John Hampden Took the King to Court Over Ship Money

John Hampden had been a leading member of the Parliamentary opposition to Charles before 1629. Deprived of the platform of the House of Commons from which to attack royal policy, in 1637 he decided to challenge in the courts the king's right to levy Ship Money annually without the consent of Parliament. He refused to pay the tax and was arrested, and in court he challenged the king to prove that the royal prerogative alone could justify the tax. The case was closely followed across the country as most people realised that if Charles won it would confirm him in his belief that he could use the prerogative to create law and levy taxes without Parliament.

Twelve judges tried the case and as all of them were appointed by the King and sat at his pleasure, most believed that the verdict was a foregone conclusion. However, when it came to it, five of the twelve found for Hampden and declared Ship Money, as currently levied, illegal. Even though Hampden had technically lost the case, many were heartened that five judges were prepared to challenge the King and it was widely reckoned that Hampden had won the moral victory.

16. In 1637 the Scots Rose in Rebellion Against Charles I

We have already noted Charles's love of order and discipline, and when he tried to impose both upon his kingdom of Scotland in 1637 it provoked rebellion. Charles demanded religious uniformity across his two kingdoms. This meant that the Presbyterian Scottish Kirk must be brought into line with the Episcopal Church of England. Charles had already tried to strengthen the hand of the Scottish bishops – he created the diocese of Edinburgh in 1633 – and in 1637 decided, with the help of the Scottish bishops and against the advice of Archbishop Laud, to impose a new prayer book on the Scottish Church, which was modelled closely upon the *Book of Common Prayer*. The reaction in Scotland was immediate and violent. In St Giles's Cathedral on 23 July 1637, a riot broke out when the dean tried to read the new service book. Demonstrations against the new prayer book spread rapidly across lowland Scotland and when Charles refused to countenance any negotiation with the critics of his policy the Scots drew up the National Covenant in early 1638.

The National Covenant was a petition signed by many thousands of Scottish Protestants who pledged themselves to defend the liberty of the Scottish Kirk and 'true religion'. While it was respectful of the king's authority, the National Covenant firmly reminded Charles that there were limits to his authority when dealing with his Scottish subjects, limits that he had exceeded when he imposed the new prayer book. For the first time since 1629 Charles faced a strong and determined opposition.

Faced with this opposition, Charles decided to raise an army, march north and teach his Scottish subjects a lesson. However, the stand taken by the Scots in opposing

Charles found a great deal of support in England where many of the political class were profoundly worried by the promotion of Arminianism in religion and Charles's use of the royal prerogative to silence opposition and rule without Parliament. Therefore, the army that marched slowly north in the spring of 1639 to face the Scots had little stomach for the fight. This was demonstrated by the fact that a truce was quickly agreed with the Scots in June 1639 called the Pacification of Berwick. This truce demonstrated Charles's military weakness and it is probable that from this point opposition leaders in England were in contact with the leaders of the Scottish resistance to coordinate policies. Meanwhile, Charles recalled Thomas Wentworth, his strongman, from Ireland where he had been Lord Deputy since 1632. Charles was confident that Wentworth's forceful personality would break all opposition.

17. The Scots Invaded England in 1640

When it became clear by the beginning of 1639 that Charles was determined to raise an army to suppress what he regarded as a rebellion in Scotland, the Covenanters quickly organised themselves. They raised an army and appointed the veteran soldier Alexander Leslie to lead it. Meanwhile, Charles arrived at York in April and proposed an ambitious strategy to beat the Covenanters involving a four-pronged attack: north from England, east from Ireland to the western Isles, west after troops had been landed in eastern Scotland and south when the loyalist clans linked up with the troops from Ireland and the east coast; the Covenanters would be crushed in this four-armed vice. Unfortunately for Charles this plan existed only on paper. In practice, he was short of money and the army he managed to raise was ill-equipped, inexperienced and badly trained. To add to Charles's woes, many Puritans in England sympathised with the Covenanters' resistance to his high-handed policies and it is certain that leading English Puritans were communicating secretly with the leaders of the Covenanting movement in Edinburgh. Despite some initial skirmishing, the main English force that assembled at Berwick soon began to disintegrate when it learnt that a determined Covenanting army was advancing through the Borders towards them. As we have seen, Charles was forced to negotiate a truce to keep the Scots out of England. But the truce satisfied no one on either side, Charles felt he had conceded too much, while the Covenanters felt he had not conceded enough, the 'First Bishops' War' had ended in humiliation for Charles and frustration for the Scots.

Charles was determined to have another go and the following year another English army marched north. The Covenanters were ready for them and decided on a pre-emptive strike into England. On 20 August 1640, Leslie and his army crossed the Tweed at Coldstream and, ignoring well-defended Berwick, marched south towards Newcastle. The only engagement of this, the 'Second Bishops' War', occurred at Newburn to the west of Newcastle where Leslie attempted to make a crossing of the Tyne. It was only a brief affair as almost as soon as battle was joined the inexperienced English soldiers turned and fled towards Newcastle. Leslie secured the crossing and then watched as the English abandoned Newcastle and withdrew to Durham; ten days after crossing the Tweed, Leslie marched into Newcastle without a shot being fired.

18. The Treaties of Ripon and London Humiliated Charles

When Leslie occupied Newcastle in August 1640 morale in the English army collapsed and it was soon clear that some sort of negotiated settlement had to be arranged. Desperate to avoid having to summon another Parliament, Charles summoned the Great Council of Peers to meet him at York. The Great Council had not met since the reign of Edward III and those peers who attended immediately urged the King to dispense with anachronistic medieval councils, sign a truce with the Scots and call a Parliament. Charles was forced to yield and, on 14 October, the Treaty of Ripon was signed between the King and the Scots. Under the terms of this treaty, the Scots were to occupy Northumberland and County Durham and, in a particularly humiliating gesture, they required Charles to foot the bill for the occupation to the tune of £850 a day; not content with that, they also demanded reparations from the English for causing the war in the first place.

Charles, now isolated and nearly bankrupt, finally agreed to summon a Parliament, which met in early November and became known as the Long Parliament. Scottish commissioners arrived shortly afterwards but negotiations dragged on through 1641 and it was not until August of that year that the Treaty of London was signed. By it Charles was obliged to accept all the changes the Scottish Covenanters had introduced since 1638, including the abolition of bishops and pay the sum of £30.000 in reparations.

19. PARLIAMENT WAS RECALLED, EVENTUALLY

The Pacification of Berwick had demonstrated the strength of opposition in Scotland and England to Charles's rule and Wentworth, created the Earl of Strafford in January 1640, advised the King to recall Parliament, the only body that could generate the finances necessary to fight a major campaign against Scotland. Strafford assured the King that he could 'manage' Parliament and bend it to the King's will. Strafford's confidence had been boosted in March 1640 when he had returned to Dublin and persuaded the Irish Parliament to vote four subsidies to raise an army with which to crush the Covenanting Scots in Ulster. This success only served to increase Strafford's confidence that the English Parliament would be as easily persuaded as the Irish – how wrong he was!

When Parliament finally reassembled at Westminster in April 1640, Strafford and the King quickly lost control of the situation. After eleven years without being able to voice their fears and frustrations, the assembled MPs erupted into action with a catalogue of grievances against Charles and his government. The man who emerged as the skilled and determined leader of the Parliamentary opposition was John Pym. Shocked by the fury of the MPs and convinced that Pym and the leading oppositionists were working with the Scottish rebels, Charles dissolved Parliament after only three weeks – this became known as the 'Short Parliament' for obvious reasons!

But what was Charles to do now? He tried to raise money to continue the war against the Scots by reverting again to obsolete prerogative taxation such as 'Coat and Conduct Money', he also issued writs for another levy of Ship Money. But now the English political nation went on strike. The gentry refused to pay their taxes unless authorised by Parliament. They also withdrew from their traditional role as the agents of local government in the counties in protest at the dissolution of the Short Parliament. The machinery of royal government began to break down in the summer of 1640.

It has been said that there could not have been a Civil War in England in 1640 because nearly everyone was united in opposition to Charles I. Certainly, the Parliament that met in November was determined not only to dismantle the machinery of the Personal Rule but also punish the King's 'evil counsellors' who had served him in the 1630s. Chief among them were Strafford and Laud, both of whom were arrested and sent to the Tower.

20. Thomas Wentworth, Lord Strafford, Was Condemned by an Act of Attainder

The trial of Strafford opened in Westminster Hall on 22 March 1641. Strafford was impeached on a charge of 'endeavouring to subvert the fundamental laws and government ... and to introduce an arbitrary and tyrannical government against law'. In particular, Strafford was accused of having encouraged the King to bring over an Irish Catholic army to subdue England. The trial did not go to plan: the charges were vague and Strafford defended himself very well; it soon looked likely that he would be acquitted. It was also known that Strafford had the support of the King, and Charles and Henrietta Maria attended each day of the trial to support Strafford. Charles had also declared that he would personally intervene to save Strafford from his enemies.

Those enemies, the opposition MPs and peers led by Pym and Warwick, could not afford to allow so dangerous a man as Strafford to escape. They abandoned the trial and instead introduced a Bill of Attainder into the Commons, which simply declared Strafford guilty of treason without the inconvenience of a trial. After acrimonious debate the bill passed the Commons on 21 April and was sent up to the Lords. To become law the attainder had to be signed by the king. Having promised to protect Strafford, Charles was now being told to sign his death warrant.

Charles tried desperately to save Strafford. He offered to take Pym and the leading oppositionists onto the Privy Council if they dropped the attainder; they refused. On 1 May the Lords passed the bill. At the same time it became known that Charles was plotting with certain army officers to seize the Tower and help Strafford escape. While all this was happening, Westminster and Whitehall were thronged with crowds demonstrating against 'Black

Tom Tyrant' and demanding his execution. Finally, in an agony of conscience, Charles signed the attainder on 10 May. Strafford was executed two days later on Tower Hill before a capacity crowd and to the accompaniment of wild rejoicing in the streets of London.

Charles never forgave himself for abandoning Strafford and, as we shall see, referred to the 'unjust sentence' he had been forced to concede at his own execution in January 1649. Many MPs and gentry, while having no love for Strafford, were nevertheless uneasy about the use of attainder to destroy him. Many of them considered his death little short of judicial murder.

21. THE CONTINUING CRISIS AT WESTMINSTER PROVOKED UNREST IN THE COUNTRY

The scenes of mob violence outside Whitehall and Westminster during the trial of Strafford were only one aspect of a progressive breakdown of law and order in London and parts of England during 1641. The London mob was active and partisan, cheering those it believed to be 'honest' and 'well affected', jeering and insulting those it did not like. Any MP or peer who criticised any aspect of the opposition programme soon discovered that they had to run the gauntlet of hostile crowds every time they entered or left Parliament. In particular, the carriages and persons of the bishops who sat in the House of Lords were abused and insulted by the crowds and there were increasing demands for the bishops to be expelled from the Lords. Violent exchanges also began to occur in the streets between individuals with differing opinions and sometimes swords were drawn. It was during the summer of 1641 that the labels 'Cavalier' and 'Roundhead' were first used as insults to traded with one's opponents.

Outside London the violence and disorder spread. The homes and property of supporters of the King were targeted, and churches where Laudian 'innovations' had been introduced were attacked and vandalised. In some cases altars were torn down, their rails chopped up and stained-glass windows smashed. In one of the worst incidents, the home of Lady Rivers at St Osyth in Essex was stormed and pillaged by a mob. Lady Rivers fled to her house at Long Melford only to have that house similarly attacked and pillaged. In the end she was rescued by officers sent by Robert Rich, Earl of Warwick, the principal landowner in Essex. Lady Rivers had been attacked because she was a Roman Catholic.

Many members of the gentry were profoundly shocked by the unrest in London and the country. It seemed that the continuing conflict between the King and Parliament was leading to the collapse of law and order. Many believed that the mobs were being secretly directed by Pym and his associates in order to intimidate their opponents. The call was now heard from many quarters to heal the breach between the King and Parliament and crack down on disorder in society.

22. The Irish Rose Up In Rebellion

In October 1641, the worst nightmare for English Protestants became a reality when the Catholic Irish rose in revolt. The rising was not spontaneous: with Strafford gone and the English distracted by the continuing conflict between the King and Parliament, the Irish felt that this was a good time to strike. Although they failed to take Dublin, the rebels soon controlled over two-thirds of Ireland, and in October 1642 they formed a parliament at Kilkenny and declared themselves to be the legitimate government of the Irish Confederation.

What provoked horror and outrage in England were the accounts of the terrible atrocities the Irish had supposedly unleashed on the Protestant settlers. Refugees who fled in the wake of the rebellion told of whole villages massacred, women raped and children impaled on spikes and roasted over fires. The atrocity stories lost nothing in the telling, but they were widely believed as they confirmed what most English Protestants believed about the Catholic Irish: that they were bloodthirsty barbarians eager to butcher all Protestants.

The King was in Edinburgh when news of the rebellion came through and he immediately offered to raise an army to take to Ireland to crush the revolt. However, Parliament was reluctant to give the King an army as they believed that there was a possibility that when in Ireland he would side with the rebels and return to England to massacre his opponents. To such a degree had trust between the King and Parliament collapsed. Parliament stated that they would only finance an army for Ireland if they could appoint all the officers, a suggestion the King rejected as an impertinent attack upon his prerogative.

Meanwhile, in Ireland, various local nobles, such as the Earl of Cork in Munster and the Earl of Ormond in

Dublin, took the lead in raising and equipping troops, often at their own expense, to resist the rebels. These forces supplemented the standing army in Ireland, a Protestant force of just over 2,000 foot and nearly 1,000 horse. In December, Sir Simon Harcourt arrived in Dublin with 1,100 foot raised by Parliament and paid for by voluntary subscriptions, and in February 1642 Colonel Monck also arrived in Dublin with a further 1,500 foot and 400 horse. In April, a Scottish army landed in Ulster, while more troops arrived from England in May. However, the problem of the appointment of officers remained between the King and Parliament. As we will see, this stalemate was exacerbated in March 1642 when Parliament passed the Militia Ordinance. In terms of Ireland, the determination to send adequate forces to suppress the rebellion faltered from the late spring of 1642 due to the stalemate over who had the authority to raise and staff military forces. Also, as England and Wales descended into civil war over the summer, both sides withdrew troops from Ireland to bolster their preparations at home.

23. THE ROYAL FAMILY WERE FORCED TO FLEE LONDON IN JANUARY 1642

By the autumn of 1641 the consensus of opinion that had prevailed in both Parliament and the country in November 1640 had vanished. Under the pressure of the trial of Strafford, the riots and disorders of the summer and the demands to radically reform the Church, a conservative reaction was setting in that felt opposition to the King had gone too far and that the continued conflict was threatening the fabric of society. In the Commons this 'moderate' party was led by Edward Hyde, Lucius Cary, Lord Falkland and Sir John Colepepper. These men now offered to work for Charles and speak for him in Parliament, and in the final months of 1641 they composed a series of highly effective royal messages and responses that presented Charles in a very favourable light as a moderate, constitutional king who regretted the continuing crisis and who was prepared to make reasonable concessions to ensure the peace and happiness of his subjects.

Aware that events seemed to be slipping out of their control, Pym and his associates introduced into the Commons the 'Grand Remonstrance' in November 1641. This enormous document – 214 clauses – sought to regain the initiative of reform by cataloguing, again, the misdeeds of Charles's government since 1625. But it went far beyond that, demanding the Parliamentary right to appoint ministers, control the army and reform the church. Not only was the Grand Remonstrance a radical and provocative document in itself, many MPs also objected to the fact that Pym had it printed and circulated outside Parliament, provoking even more mob violence.

The Grand Remonstrance was presented to the King on 1 December and his reply, issued on the 23rd and probably written by Edward Hyde, was a model of constitutional restraint. Quietly, but firmly repeating a moderate, conservative line based on respect for the law and traditional practice, it seemed that with Charles rebranded as a moderate, constitutional monarch he might be able to outflank the opposition.

However, there was a problem, namely, the character of Charles himself. The Ladybird book *Oliver Cromwell* (one of a series of books published for children) states boldly that 'King Charles was a very stupid man'. Certainly he was an indecisive man who often tried to pursue two different policies at the same time, usually ensuring in the process that neither policy was successful. While Hyde and Falkland were trying to present Charles as a constitutional king, others at court, including the Queen, were urging him to assert his authority and use force against his opponents and strike them down.

Thus, on 3 January 1642, Charles formally impeached Lord Kimbolton and five MPs, including Pym and Hampden, on charges of treason. The following day Charles went to Westminster with an armed guard and entered the House of Commons. Taking the speaker's chair, he demanded the arrest of the five members; they were not present. Having been forewarned of the King's intentions, the five MPs and Kimbolton had gone into hiding with their friends in the City. When he realised that his plan had failed Charles remarked, 'Well, I see all the birds are flown'. He had no option but to withdraw with the indignant MPs on their feet shouting 'Privilege! Privilege!' as he left. The next day Charles's failure was compounded when the Common Council of the City of London refused to hand over the fugitives. Charles drove back to Whitehall through hostile crowds and his humiliation was complete.

The botched attempt to arrest Kimbolton and the five MPs united the opposition as never before. Now the mobs in London were joined by the trained bands who gathered to protect Parliament against any further royal aggression, and men began to arm themselves. Frightened for his own and his family's safety, Charles left London in haste on 10 January. It is said that their flight was so precipitate that no preparations had been made for their arrival that evening at Hampton Court, no fires had been lit, no beds aired or food provided. The royal family were obliged to share one bed in an effort to keep warm! The same day, Pym and his colleagues returned in triumph to Westminster, where they were given a hero's welcome. The events of January 1642 put both the King and Parliament on the slippery slope to war.

24. The Militia Ordinance Was a Major Step on the Road to War

Both the King and Parliament agreed that an army should be raised and sent to Ireland to suppress the rebellion, and a Militia Bill was proposed in December 1641. Unfortunately, neither the King nor Parliament trusted the other with control of such an army. Charles suspected that if Parliament gained control of the army the opposition would use it against him, while many in Parliament believed that if Charles commanded an army he might unite with the Irish rebels and turn on Parliament. The bill eventually presented to the Commons proposed that Parliament rather than the King should nominate the senior officers. This was a direct attack upon the royal prerogative and Charles refused his assent to the bill.

However, in March 1642 Parliament took the radical step of issuing the Militia Bill as an ordinance. They claimed that in the interests of national security they could act independently of the King and that the Militia Ordinance had the force of law, even though it had not received the royal assent. Parliament also claimed the right to appoint the Lords-Lieutenant in the counties, again, another direct attack on the prerogative. Charles immediately issued a declaration condemning the Militia Ordinance and denouncing the right of Parliament to appoint Lords-Lieutenant as unconstitutional, he also forbade all in authority to obey Parliament's ordinance.

Subsequently, Charles issued his own orders, called the Commission of Array, to the Lords-Lieutenant ordering them to raise and equip the militia in their respective counties. By the early summer of 1642 gentlemen across England and Wales were faced with two contradictory orders to mobilise the counties's armed forces, one from Parliament, the other from the King; which one were they to obey? For many this was the point at which they were forced to make a choice and declare an allegiance. The attempts by local officers to enforce either the Militia Ordinance or the Commission of Array provoked the first serious clashes of the Civil War.

25. ENGLAND SPLITS INTO ROYALIST AND PARLIAMENTARIAN AREAS

By the summer of 1642 England had begun to split apart into Royalist and Parliamentarian regions. Broadly speaking, the south-east, London and East Anglia were Parliamentarian, while the south-west, Wales and the north were for the King, with the Thames Valley and the Midlands as disputed territory. Naturally, we should not take these divisions too literally or believe that every single individual within these regions were universally committed to one side or the other. Within each region there would be a range of opinion – Royalist, Parliamentarian and neutral – and even in areas effectively secured for one side, such as Parliamentarian East Anglia, there were many Royalist sympathisers. What tended to happen was that those out of sympathy with the dominant power in their region either left to join the other side, or kept their heads down and their mouths shut hoping that the enemy would not find them out!

What is also noticeable from the division of England is that Parliament controlled the wealthiest part of the country. London, East Anglia and the south-east, then as now, were the most densely populated and prosperous parts of England. Parliament also controlled London with its arsenal in the Tower, the Mint and the financial resources of the City and the Port of London. Parliament also controlled much of the coastline from Yorkshire round to Southampton on the south coast and with most of the fleet under their control they could make it very difficult for the Royalists to land troops and supplies from the Continent. By contrast, the King would find it far harder to find the long-term resources to fight a long war. He needed a swift victory to take advantage of his initial superiority in men and resources.

26. Each Side Sought to Raise Armies in the Summer of 1642

As the spring and summer of 1642 progressed, both sides spoke of peace while preparing for war. After the royal family left London it was decided that the Queen should journey to the Netherlands, with jewellery and plate that included some of the crown jewels, with which to raise loans on their security and buy weapons, powder and recruit troops for the King. Meanwhile, Parliament appointed Sir John Hotham to be Governor of Hull, a vital port on the Yorkshire coast and the largest arsenal in northern England. Parliament instructed Hotham not to admit the King to Hull without their express permission. In April, Charles arrived before Hull and demanded entry; Hotham refused. Frustrated at finding the gates barred against him and without sufficient forces to either storm or besiege the town, Charles had no option but to withdraw, defeated and furious. The King moved to York and in August raised his standard at Nottingham, but still recruits failed to appear in significant numbers to swell the royal army. It was only when Charles marched west to Chester and the Welsh border in September that recruits finally began to pour in. From then on, the major source of recruits for the Royalist field army was to be Wales and the Welsh Marches.

Meanwhile, Parliament had been busy consolidating its hold on London, the south-east and East Anglia. Together with the London Trained Bands and the County Militias, Parliament found a ready source of recruits from East Anglia. As England split apart in the spring and summer of 1642 both sides consolidated the areas they controlled as the sources for long-term recruitment and support.

27. ANTHONY WOOD DESCRIBES THE ENTHUSIASM FOR SOLDIERING AMONG THE YOUNG MEN OF OXFORD

Anthony Wood (1632–95) was an Oxford historian and antiquary who wrote a great history of the university. Writing in the third person, he described the scene in Oxford during the first summer of the Civil War when men were busy arming themselves with any old equipment they happened to have lying around, when the undergraduates drilled in college quads and schoolboys found watching the soldiers far more entertaining than swotting over their Latin grammars.

Mr Wood's father had then armour or furniture for one man, namely a helmet, a back and breastpiece, a pike and a musket, and other appurtenances: and the eldest of his men-servants (for he had then three at least) named Thomas Burnham did appear in those arms, when the scholars and privileged men trained; and when he could not train, as being taken up with business, the next servant did train: and much ado there was to keep Thomas Wood, the eldest son, then a student at Christ Church and a youth of about 18 years of age, from putting on the said armour and to train among the scholars.

The said scholars and privileged men did sometimes train in New College quadrangle, in the eye of Dr Robert Pink, the deputy Vice-Chancellor, then Warden of the said college. And it being a novel matter, there was no holding of the schoolboys in their school in the cloister from seeing and following them. And Mr Wood remembered well, that some of them were so besotted with the training and activity and gaiety therein of some young scholars, as being in a longing condition to be one of the train, that they could never be brought to their books again. It was a great disturbance to the youth of the city, and Mr Wood's father foresaw that if his sons were not removed from Oxford they would be spoiled.

Adair, J. *By the Sword Divided: Eyewitnesses of the English Civil War.*
(London: Book Club Associates, 1983), p. 74.

28. Many Were Reluctant to Choose Sides

As with most civil wars there are usually only a relatively small number of committed zealots on either side who spring to arms totally convinced of the righteousness of their cause. Most people in England in the spring and summer of 1642 watched the slide into war with fear and incomprehension and most tried to delay taking sides until the last possible moment. A point of decision for some came with the passing of the Militia Ordinance at the beginning of March, particularly when the King subsequently issued a strongly worded condemnation of it. Presented with a demand to take up arms under the ordinance, individuals like Sir Thomas Knyvett, as you can see below, had to decide whether to comply, refuse or withdraw, hoping that they could avoid a decision. A further point of decision came in June when the King issued his Commissions of Array. Now there were two separate instructions ordering them to muster for either the King or Parliament. Which one would they obey, or would it be wiser to try to avoid both? As the Devon magistrates said in a petition to the King in August 1642, 'In how hard a condition are we, while a twofold obedience, like twins in the womb, strives to be born to both.'* The summer of 1642 was a period of military preparation, but it was also a time when men and women wrestled with their consciences and agonised over the best course of action to take.

Here is an extract from a letter Sir Thomas Knyvett wrote to his wife about his dilemma:

> Oh sweet heart, I am now in a great straight what to do. Walking this other morning at Westminster, Sir John Potts, with Commissary Muttford, saluted me with a commission from the Lord of Warwick, to take upon me

(by virtue of an Ordinance of Parliament) my company and command again. I was surprised what to do, whether to take or refuse. 'Twas no place to dispute, so I took it and desired sometime to advise upon it. I had not received this many hours, but I met with a declaration point blank against it by the King.

This distraction made me advise with some understanding men what condition I stand in, which is no other than a great many men of quality do. What further commands we shall receive to put this ordinance in execution, if they run in a way that trenches upon my obedience against the King, I shall do according to my conscience, and this is the resolution of all honest men that I can speak with.*

*Devon Quarter Sessions. Petition to the King, 16 August 1642. *Letter from Sir Thomas Knyvett to Lady Knyvett, 18 May 1642. Both in John Morrill, *The Revolt of the Provinces: Conservatives and Radicals in the English Civil War 1630–1650* (London: Longman, 1980), pp. 162 and 136.

29. PRINCE RUPERT WAS BORN IN PRAGUE

One man who had no doubt as to which side he was on was Prince Rupert (1619–82) one of the most glamorous and swashbuckling of Royalist commanders. His father was Frederick V, Elector Palatine of the Rhine (1596–1632) and his mother was the Princess Elizabeth (1596–1662), daughter of James VI and I and sister of Charles I. Their capital was at Heidelberg on the Rhine, so why was Rupert born over 300 miles away in Prague? The Palatinate was part of the Holy Roman Empire, a patchwork quilt of principalities, archbishoprics and imperial cities across what is today Germany. All the rulers of the Empire owed allegiance to the Emperor in Vienna but had a great deal of independence in the government of their own states. Seven of the princes were, like Frederick, electors, when the Emperor died or abdicated they 'elected' his successor, although since the mid-fifteenth century, and with one short exception in the eighteenth century, the emperors were always members of the Habsburg family.

The Protestant Reformation had begun in the Empire 100 years before Rupert was born and by the early seventeenth century the Empire was split between Catholic and Protestant states, with the Emperor in Vienna remaining staunchly Catholic. Tensions mounted between Catholics and Protestants and in 1618 the Protestant nobility of Bohemia rebelled against the Emperor, seizing and throwing two of his representatives out of windows of Hradschin Castle in what came to be known as 'the defenestration of Prague'. (The officials survived their fall because they landed on a large rubbish heap in the Castle courtyard.) The Bohemian nobility then invited Frederick and Elizabeth to become the King and Queen of Bohemia because Frederick was one of the leading Protestant princes of the Empire. They accepted the invitation and arrived in Prague during the autumn of 1619, Rupert was born on 18 December.

But Frederick and Rupert were not to remain long in Prague. The Emperor raised a Catholic army to suppress the rebellion and, on 8 November 1620, defeated Frederick and the Protestants at the battle of the White Mountain and occupied Prague. Frederick and Elizabeth, with their children, were forced to flee and their brief tenure of the Bohemian throne earnt them the title 'The Winter King and Queen'. Meanwhile, Spanish allies of the Emperor invaded the Palatinate, occupying and sacking Heidelberg. These events caused the Protestant princes of the Empire to combine to resist the joint Habsburg-Spanish assault, which was to escalate when the French entered the war against the Spanish-Habsburg alliance. This war, which devastated large parts of central Europe, was not concluded until 1648 and is known as the Thirty Years War – for obvious reasons! Unable to return home after leaving Prague, Frederick and his family went into exile in the Netherlands and it was here that Rupert spent his youth.

30. Henrietta Maria Was Called 'Her She-Majesty, Generalissima'

As we have seen, early in 1642 Henrietta Maria travelled to the Spanish Netherlands and Holland and was to spend nearly a year at the Hague buying arms and recruiting soldiers for the royal cause. Ostensibly she was there to oversee the marriage of her eldest daughter, Mary, to Prince William of Orange, she was also accompanied by Prince Rupert and his younger brother, Maurice. While in the Netherlands Henrietta Maria appointed Rupert commander of the Royalist cavalry and she eventually returned to England in February 1643. Most of the English navy had sided with Parliament, so Henrietta Maria and her small fleet had to try and avoid enemy ships while crossing the Channel, they eventually landed at Bridlington on the Yorkshire coast. But even now she was not safe because Parliamentary ship began to bombard the port and the Queen and her ladies were forced to flee the town and take cover among the sand dunes as the shot whistled over their heads, but not before running back to her lodgings to rescue her pet dog, Mitte. Henrietta Maria holds the rare distinction of being the only English monarch ever to be fired on by the 'Royal' navy!

Now all she had to do was march with her small army, the arms and supplies, from Bridlington to the Royalist capital at Oxford across enemy-held territory! Initially she made for York and waited there until, by the summer, it was considered safe enough to continue. The Queen, who now called herself 'Her She-Majesty Generalissima', rode out of York at the head of her army and train. She headed for the Royalist stronghold of Newark and then turned south. Charles rode north from Oxford and met up with the wife he had not seen for nearly eighteenth months at Edgehill. The King and Queen, complete with men and supplies, made a triumphal entry into Oxford on 14 July.

31. Rupert Pledged His Support for His Uncle

We left Rupert and his family in the Netherlands after they were driven out of Prague and Heidelberg was captured by the Spanish and Rupert was to grow up there. His father, Frederick, died on campaign in 1632 and Rupert's elder brother, Charles Louis, became the new elector in exile. Exile and the need to make his own way in the world were to be dominant themes in Rupert's life. During the 1630s, Rupert and Charles Louis visited their aunt and uncle, Henrietta Maria and Charles, in England, and by the time he was eighteen Rupert had decided on a military career and joined the Protestant forces besieging Breda in the autumn of 1637.

But his first military career was to be short-lived. The following year Rupert was captured by Imperial forces at the battle of Vlotho in north Germany and he spent the following two years as a prisoner of war in Linz Castle. It was to help relieve the monotony of imprisonment that Thomas Howard, Earl of Arundel and family friend, sent Rupert a white hunting poodle as a gift. Rupert called the dog Boy, and they became inseparable. As we will see, Boy was to become something of a celebrity through Parliamentarian propaganda during the Civil War.

Meanwhile, in October 1641, Charles I persuaded the Emperor to release his nephew, and in February 1642 Rupert and his younger brother, Maurice, sailed to England to pledge their allegiance to their uncle in the mounting crisis. As we have seen, Rupert and Maurice accompanied Henrietta Maria on her visit to the Hague to buy supplies and raise troops for the Royal cause. Rupert and Maurice returned to England in July 1642 with supplies and volunteers and joined the King at Nottingham. Charles confirmed Rupert's commission as commander of the Royalist horse and conferred on him the Garter. Rupert and Maurice were also present when Charles raised his standard on 22 August 1642. Throughout that fateful summer Rupert was active raising and training the cavalry, his dash and enthusiasm soon paid dividends in terms of recruits and on 23 September Rupert and his men scored a notable success when they scattered a Parliamentarian force at the Battle of Powicke Bridge, near Worcester. The 'battle' was actually nothing more than a skirmish, but it confirmed Rupert's reputation as a successful and charismatic cavalry commander. By the time Rupert prepared to fight the battle of Edgehill he had between 2,500 and 2,800 cavalrymen at his disposal.

32. The Battle of Edgehill Was the First Major Engagement of the Civil War

We saw how the majority of recruits for the King's army came from Wales and the Welsh Marches, by the end of September 1642 Charles had raised fifteen regiments of foot, eight of horse and a regiment of dragoons. Meanwhile, Parliament raised an army from London and Essex of twelve regiments of foot, six of horse and a regiment of dragoons, command was given to the Earl of Essex who personally raised a lifeguard regiment of cuirassiers. Essex's first plan was to march north to Nottingham, but on discovering Charles was on the Welsh border he mustered his army at Northampton and marched west towards Worcester, where his advance troop of cavalry were scattered by Rupert at Powick Bridge.

Charles believed that his best hope of a quick victory was to advance on London and when Essex realised that this was the King's intention he set off in pursuit. On the morning of 22 October both sides discovered that they were only a few miles apart and the Royalists turned to fight at Edgehill in southern Warwickshire. The two armies were fairly evenly matched, although the Royalist cavalry was more experienced. When the battle was joined at around 3 p.m. on the 23rd most people believed that one decisive battle would decide the issues between the King and Parliament.

The battle began well for the Royalists: Rupert's cavalry charged on both flanks and broke through the Parliamentarian ranks. If Rupert's cavalry had been able to regroup and turn on the rear of the Parliamentarian centre, things would soon have become desperate for the infantry, but instead the cavalry charged on across the battlefield, pursuing fleeing Parliamentarians and raiding the baggage train. Rupert's cavalry were brave and enthusiastic, but their lack of discipline often cost the Royalists dear!

Meanwhile, the infantry closed in hand-to-hand fighting, the Royalists were slowly pushed back and at one point the royal standard was captured. It looked as if the Royalist infantry might break under the pressure but at this point Rupert's cavalry returned to the battlefield and bolstered the Royalist position, recapturing the royal standard in the process. By now the light was fading and both exhausted armies drew apart but remained on the battlefield retrieving their dead and tending the wounded. However, Charles still commanded the road to London and when Essex withdrew to Warwick, Charles resumed his advance on London. Rupert's cavalry reached Brentford on 12 November, where they stormed and sacked the town. The following day, when the Royalist infantry caught up with Rupert, the advance resumed and the Royalists advanced as far as Turnham Green – now a stop on the District and Piccadilly lines in west London. While all this was happening, Essex had returned to London and, with his army, the London militia trained bands supported by thousands of civilians streamed out to Turnham Green in a great effort to stop the Royalists – and stop them they did! Having failed to take London and with winter coming on, Charles withdrew back through Reading to Oxford, which became the Royalist capital for the remainder of the war. The battle of Edgehill was a shock for most people, preparing for war is different from actually fighting a war and the fact that Englishmen were now killing Englishmen, fathers were fighting sons, and brothers killing brothers was seen as a great and terrible tragedy, particularly as it was also now clear that the war would not be over by Christmas.

33. Sir Edmund Verney – Priest Puncher and Reluctant Royalist

Sir Edmund (1590–1642) was born at Pendley Manor, Buckinghamshire, and was knighted by James VI and I in 1612. He was sent on a diplomatic mission to Madrid and, on his return, entered the household of Henry, Prince of Wales. When Henry died in 1612, Verney became a Gentleman of the Privy Chamber to Charles, Duke of York, and from 1620 made his home at Middle Claydon, Buckinghamshire. In 1623, Verney accompanied Charles and the Duke of Buckingham on their visit to Spain to woo the Spanish infanta. Apparently, while in Spain, Verney intervened to save a dying Englishman from the unwelcome attentions of a Catholic priest who was hoping for a deathbed conversion. It is claimed that when the priest persisted Verney punched him in the face; needless to say, this did not go down well with the Spanish!

Verney was an MP in both the 1625 and the 1629 Parliaments as well as the Short Parliament of April–May 1640 and the Long Parliament, which met the following November. In Parliament, Verney was often critical of Charles's policies during the Personal Rule and consistently opposed the Arminian religious practices sponsored by Archbishop Laud. However, with the approach of Civil War, during the summer of 1642, Verney's conscience would not allow him to betray his king and he reluctantly enlisted in the King's army, being made standard bearer at Edgehill. Verney's struggle with his conscience are summed up in a famous letter to a friend in which he wrote:

> I do not like... the quarrel, and do heartily wish that the King would yield and consent to what they desire,

so that my conscience is only concerned in honour and in gratitude to follow my master. I have eaten his bread, and served him nearly thirty years, and will not do so base a thing as to forsake him; and choose rather to lose my life—which I am sure to do—to preserve and defend those things which are against my conscience to preserve and defend.*

Verney's eldest son, Ralph, sided with Parliament, but went into exile in 1643 rather than take the Presbyterian covenant. As Verney's daughter remarked at the beginning of the war, 'indeed, the world now account[s] it policy for the father to be one side and the son on the other.'**

Verney was killed during the battle of Edgehill and his body never recovered. There is a tradition that when the royal standard was recovered Verney's severed hand was still clutching it tightly.

Sir Edmund Verney's experience illustrates both the agonies of doubt some went through over which side to support, as well as the way the war split families and saw fathers fighting sons and brother killing brother.

*Hunt, T. *The English Civil War at First Hand* (London: Phoenix, 2003), pp. 87–88.

** Susan E. Whyman, 'Verney, Sir Edward (1590–1642)', *Oxford Dictionary of National Biography* (Oxford University Press, 2004; online ed., May 2009). [http://www/oxforddnb.com/view/article/28228, accessed 10 March 2017]

34. The Year 1643 Was a Good One for the Royalists

Despite the failure to take London, the campaigning season of 1643 opened with the Royalists doing well. Firmly established in Oxford, the Royalist field army expanded throughout the winter of 1642–43, it was well paid, well officered and its cavalry was superior to that of Parliament, commanded by the King's dashing nephew, Prince Rupert. Sir Ralph Hopton in the south-west and the Marquess of Newcastle in the north made great gains for the King, Newcastle securing control of most of Yorkshire with his victory at the battle of Adwalton Moor on 30 June. Hopton had defeated the Earl of Stamford at the battle of Stratton on 16 May. In April, as we have seen, Henrietta Maria landed at Bridlington with arms and money raised on the Continent for the Royalist cause. The high point of Royalist success came on 26 July when Prince Rupert took Bristol, England's second city.

Meanwhile, divisions were emerging in Parliament between a 'war party' and the moderates. The war party wanted to prosecute the war vigorously, defeat the King and then dictate a peace to him. They were also critical of the command of the Parliamentary forces, accusing the Earl of Essex of not having the stomach to beat the King. The war party was faced by a larger group who were profoundly uncomfortable with the possible implications of fighting the King and hoped for some sort of negotiated settlement, which would somehow end the war quickly before any more damage could be done. However, their initial overtures to Charles in what became known as the Treaty of Oxford were brushed aside by the King who was confident that his military forces would prevail.

35. Ann Fanshawe Describes Life in Royalist Oxford in 1643

Ann Fanshawe, née Harrison (1625–80), came from a solidly Royalist family; her brother, William, joined the King at Nottingham and her father was arrested by Parliament, threatened with transportation and his estates sequestered. This explains the poverty of the family when they moved to Oxford the following year and her memoirs, written many years later, give an impression of what life was like in Royalist Oxford:

My father commanded my sister and myself to come to him to Oxford where the court then was; but we, that had till that hour lived in great plenty and great order, found ourselves like fishes out of water and the scene so changed that we knew not at all how to act any part but obedience; for from as good houses as any gentleman of England had we come to a baker's house in an obscure street, and from rooms well furnished to lie in a very bad bed in a garret, to one dish of meat and that not the best ordered: no money, for we were as poor as Job, nor clothes more than a man or two brought in their cloak bags.

We had the perpetual discourse of losing and gaining of towns and men; at the windows the sad spectacle of war, sometimes plague, sometimes sicknesses of other kind, by reason of so many people being packed together, as I believe there never was before of that quality; always wants, yet I must needs say that most bore it with a martyr-like cheerfulness. For my part I began to think we should all, like Abraham, live in tents all the days of our lives.*

Ann married her staunchly Royalist second cousin, Richard Fanshawe, in 1644, and as the Royalist cause collapsed in

1645 Ann and Richard followed Prince Charles into exile. Apart from bearing twenty-three children, of whom only three survived into adulthood, in later life Ann compiled a cookery book which, it is claimed, contains the first recorded recipe in England for ice cream.

*Adair, J. *By the sword Divided: Eyewitnesses of the English Civil War* (London: Book Club Associates, 1983), pp. 79–80.

36. The Civil War Divided Friends, Families and Communities

Sir William Waller was a prominent Parliamentarian commander. He wrote to his friend, Sir Ralph Hopton, who was an equally prominent Royalist commander. Civil War divides friends in the same way as it divides families and communities and we can see some of the pain of those divisions in Waller's letter:

To my noble friend Sir Ralph Hopton at Wells.

Sir, The experience I have had of your worth and the happiness I have enjoyed in your friendship, are wounding consideration when I look upon this present distance between us. Certainly my affections to you are so unchangeable that hostility itself cannot violate my friendship to your person, but I must be true to the cause wherein I serve. The old limitation usque ad aras [up to the altars] holds still, and where my conscience is interested all other obligations are swallowed up. I should most gladly wait on you, according to your desire, but that I look upon you as you are engaged in that party beyond a possibility of retreat and consequently incapable of being wrought upon by any persuasion. And I know the conference could never be so close between us that it would take wind and receive a construction to my dishonour.

That great God which is the searcher of my heart, knows with what a sad sense I go upon this service and with what a perfect hatred I detest this war without an enemy, but I look upon it as an opus domini, which is enough to silence all passion in me. The God of peace in his good time send us peace and in the meantime fit us to receive it. We are both upon the stage and must act those parts that are assigned us in this tragedy. Let us do it in a way of honour and without personal animosities. Whatever the issue be, I shall never willingly relinquish the dear title of your most affectionate friend and faithful servant, William Waller.

Bath 16th June 1643.*

*Adair, J, *By the sword divided: eyewitnesses of the English Civil War* (London: Book Club Associates, 1983), p. 92.

37. WAGING WAR IS EXPENSIVE

War is expensive, and as the conflict dragged on both sides adopted measures to ensure a steady flow of cash with which to buy arms and pay their troops. Initially, the King had the advantage. His appeal for money to the gentry brought in substantial amount of cash. Also, the colleges of the University of Oxford donated a great deal of money and plate to the King's cause. The University of Cambridge would have followed suit but, as we will see, was prevented by the intervention of Cromwell. The Royalists also tried to tax the counties under their control, setting up associations along the lines of the Parliamentarian Eastern Association, to facilitate the raising of money and resources. The armies of both sides also lived off the land, a fact that often caused real friction with local communities. Soldiers would be billeted with local families, troops would requisition, and in many cases simply steal, horses, livestock, hay, wheat etc. Sometimes receipts were issued to the locals for the goods requisition, but it soon became clear that these receipts were not really worth the paper they were written on!

Initially, Parliament found it harder to raise money or elicit donations from its supporters and in the early days of the war often found it hard to pay its troops. However, throughout 1643 a series of measures adopted by Parliament greatly improved their financial position. An Excise Tax was introduced on commodities to fund the war. In Parliamentary controlled counties a county committee was set up to oversee the war effort and to raise taxes. Often deeply unpopular with the locals, the county committees were backed up by the army and could effectively impose Parliamentary instructions and collected substantial amounts of money. In particular they were required to collect the assessment. Each county under Parliament's control was assessed for a monthly tax, which was the county committee's responsibility to collect and send onto Parliament. Again, the assessment was deeply unpopular, but it was collected. Parliament also set up a system of sequestration and composition. This meant that the estates of their enemies were confiscated (sequestered) and the income diverted to Parliament. If the owner wanted his estate back he had to pay a fine (composition). The threat of sequestration was also a very effective way of keeping disaffected gentry under control in Parliamentary dominated areas.

As the war turned against the Royalists in 1644, they found it harder to continue to raise money. As counties passed to the control of Parliament, their revenues were denied to the King and flowed into the coffers of Parliament. The King's troops were increasingly obliged to depend upon free quarter, which only served to make the Royalist troop deeply unpopular. The reliance on donations was only a short-term measure, whereas the excise, the assessment and sequestration provided large amounts of revenue on a long-term basis.

38. PARLIAMENT CLAIMED THAT PRINCE RUPERT'S DOG WAS GIVEN TO HIM BY THE DEVIL

We have seen that Boy had been given to Rupert by the Earl of Arundel while he was a prisoner of war in Linz. Boy and Rupert became inseparable and Boy accompanied Rupert into battle. Rupert inspired fear in his enemies, Parliamentary propaganda accused Rupert of using 'German' terror tactics in England learnt during his service in the Thirty Years War. In pamphlets and broadsides, Parliament called him 'Prince Robber' and claimed that he relished sacking and burning towns, that he encouraged his men to slaughter civilians, including women and children, and that he was solely intent on plunder. In an age that believed in witchcraft, Parliamentarian propagandists also claimed that Rupert was in league with the Devil and that Boy was his familiar, given to him by the Devil to protect him in battle and aid him in his devilish work. Boy was killed at the battle of Marston Moor on 2 July 1644 and Parliament soon published a gleeful account of how Rupert had lost his satanic assistant.

39. Cromwell Formed a New Sort of Army in the Eastern Association

We have seen how many people agonised over whether to support Parliament or the King, but one person who was never in any doubt where his loyalties lay was Oliver Cromwell. With the upturn in his fortunes in the later 1620s and armed with a deep Puritan conviction, Cromwell was elected MP for Huntingdon in 1628. In Parliament, he joined with the opposition to Charles I's policies and to the growth of Arminian influence in the church.

Throughout the 1630s Cromwell maintained contact with the Puritan opposition to the King and in 1640 was elected to the Long Parliament as one of the MPs for Cambridge. During the summer of 1642 Cromwell raised a troop of horse in Huntingdon and, in August, led this troop into Cambridge to prevent the Colleges sending their plate to the King. Cromwell's prompt action effectively secured Cambridgeshire, Huntingdonshire and the Isle of Ely for Parliament. He was present at Edgehill where he was impressed by the quality of the Royalist cavalry compared to that available to Parliament.

In December 1642, Parliament created the Eastern Association. This was formed initially from the counties of Norfolk, Suffolk, Essex, Hertfordshire, Cambridgeshire and the Isle of Ely. The following year Huntingdonshire and Lincolnshire were added to the Association. The task of the Association was to mobilise the region for the Parliamentary war effort. With its headquarters in Cambridge the Association raised taxes, supplied men for the army, negotiated with the county committees in the member counties and suppressed Royalists. The military command of the Association was given to the Earl of Manchester, and Cromwell was, from the beginning, an important figure, being commissioned as a colonel in the Association's army. In March 1643, Cromwell seized the ports of Lowestoft and Kings Lynn for Parliament, in April he seized Peterborough and advanced into Lincolnshire. In July he fought at Gainsborough and was made Governor of Ely. At the Battle of Winceby on 11 October, Cromwell joined forces for the first time with Sir Thomas Fairfax. Together they defeated the Royalists and recovered most of Lincolnshire for Parliament.

The following year Cromwell was promoted to the rank of Lieutenant-General of Horse and fought at the battle of Marston Moor on 2 July, where his 'Ironsides' proved more than a match for Rupert and the Royalist cavalry. The performance of Cromwell's Ironsides at Marston Moor vindicated Cromwell's policy of turning the army of the Eastern Association into a disciplined, professional force, which could take the war successfully to the enemy. He also insisted on a measure of ideological commitment, particularly from his officers, who should believe in the cause for which they fought. By 1644 Cromwell was emerging not just as one of the most prominent Parliamentarian generals but also as a leading Independent in the emerging split between Independents and Presbyterians in Parliament. Tensions which were to come to a head in Cromwell's clash with Manchester in November 1644 and the subsequent formation of the New Model Army.

40. Parliament Signed a Treaty With the Scots

Despite Royalist successes in 1643, a development occurred in August that boded ill for the future when Parliament sent commissioners north to negotiate a military alliance with the Scots. Such an alliance had been proposed by John Pym months before and was built upon shared religious and political sympathies, which had emerged during the Bishops' Wars. Four Parliamentary Commissioners and two clergymen were sent to Edinburgh and negotiations proved so straightforward that the proposals were ready for the approval of Parliament by the end of the month. Known as the 'Solemn League and Covenant', the Scots agreed to send an army into northern England to support Parliament and engage the Royalist, in return, Parliament agreed to impose the Presbyterian Church system.

The latter was easier said than done. To begin with, it was impossible to see how this could be achieved in Wales and Ireland without using overwhelming military force to coerce the people. Of greater immediate concern was the opposition of the emerging Independent groups within the Parliamentarian camp to any attempt to impose a uniform, coercive national Church, whether Anglican or Presbyterian. In 1644, Parliament decreed that all office holders whether in the military or the state had to sign the Covenant to retain their office; many refused and resigned. Tensions also developed between the Scots and the English Parliament over the nature of the Church that would be established, with the Scots accusing the English of being lax in their interpretation of Presbyterian discipline. In particular, they condemned the fact that Parliament declared the Church should be wholly under the control of Parliament; to the Scots Covenanters this was heresy and fatally compromised the independence of the General Assembly of the Church.

41. THOMAS FAIRFAX EMERGED AS A LEADING PARLIAMENTARIAN COMMANDER

Thomas Fairfax was born at Denton Hall, nearly Otley, Yorkshire, on 17 January 1612; he was the eldest son of Ferdinando, 2nd Lord Fairfax. After Cambridge and two years at the Inns of Court, he volunteered to fight for the Protestant cause in the Netherlands. He also took part in the Bishops' Wars of 1639–40, for which he was knighted in January 1640. Unlike most Yorkshire gentry, Fairfax and his father supported Parliament and in June 1642 he was chosen to present a petition to the King urging moderation and reconciliation; Charles refused to receive the petition. When war broke out, Ferdinando commanded the small Parliamentarian army in Yorkshire with Thomas as his second in command.

Fairfax was to see a great deal of action in Yorkshire and, as we have seen, in October 1642 he joined forces with Cromwell and forces of the Eastern Association at the battle of Winceby, he then took part in a successful attack on the town of Gainsborough. This was to be the beginning of a very successful collaboration between Fairfax and Cromwell. Fairfax also played a major role in the northern campaign in alliance with the Scots, which culminated in the battle of Marston Moor and the capture of York.

His military reputation made Fairfax a natural choice as Lord General of the New Model Army. His admiration for Cromwell's military skills made him petition Parliament to exempt Cromwell from the demands of the 'Self-Denying Ordinance' and Fairfax appointed him Lieutenant-General of horse and his second in command. Together, Fairfax and Cromwell delivered the fatal blow to the Royalist cause at the battle of Naseby in June 1645, before advancing into the South-west where Fairfax defeated the Royalist forces. His last campaign of the first Civil War was to command the siege of Oxford, which surrendered in June 1646.

Fairfax was a fine soldier, but he was not a politician and took little part in the clashes between the army and Parliament or the Putney Debates of 1647. But when the second Civil War broke out in 1648, Fairfax marched against the Royalists in Kent and Essex and defeated them at the siege of Colchester. However, the radicalisation of the army was not to Fairfax's taste and Pride's Purge and the trial of the King were the points at which Fairfax parted company with 'the Good Old Cause'. He took no part in the King's trial and execution and in 1650 resigned his commission as Lord General, to be replaced by Cromwell.

Fairfax retired to his estates at Nun Appleton in Yorkshire and took no further part in events until, in 1659, as the country spiralled into chaos after the death of Cromwell, he began a correspondence with General Monck in Scotland in which he advocated the restoration of Parliamentary authority over the army. Monck and Fairfax may also have discussed the restoration of the monarchy. When Monck marched into England on 1 January 1660, Fairfax took control of York and ensured that most of the Parliamentarian forces in Yorkshire threw their support behind Monck. Fairfax supported the Restoration, became an MP for Yorkshire and even lent Charles II the horse he rode to his coronation; Fairfax died in 1671.

Thomas Fairfax, nicknamed 'Black Tom' because of his black hair and swarthy looks, was a courageous and experienced soldier and even the Royalists acknowledged that he was an honourable opponent who observed the rules of war. The one exception was at Colchester, where Fairfax conducted the siege with great ferocity and had the Royalist commanders Sir George Lisle and Sir Charles Lucas court martialled and shot after they surrendered. However, the cities of York and Oxford have good reason to be grateful to Fairfax, in both places he worked hard to restrain his troops after these cities surrendered from going on the rampage, plundering and destroying the medieval glass in York Minster or ransacking the College chapels and libraries in Oxford.

42. Parliament Was Increasingly Split Between Presbyterians and Independents

Mention has already been made of the emerging split within the Parliamentarian movement between Independents and Presbyterians, with Cromwell as one of the leading Independents. This split originated in a fundamental disagreement within the Puritan movement over the position of the institutional church. Was the church the structure established by law to which all should be made to belong, or was it a voluntary community of true believers? The logic of justification by faith alone, election and predestination, etc., led many to argue that an institutional church was unnecessary as all true Christians had to come to God in their own way with the Bible as their only guide. Others argued that the institutional church was necessary to guide against heresy, maintain social discipline and preach orthodox doctrine. This immediately raised the question of who decided what was orthodox doctrine and how it should be enforced.

During the Civil War these two opposing views were expressed by the Independents and the Presbyterians. The Presbyterians, following the example of the Scottish Kirk, believed in the necessity of an exclusive, institutional church supported by law, to which all were required to belong. The Independents, who came to dominate the New Model Army, rejected this view, insisting that each Christian was free, within certain limits, to follow their conscience and to seek God where they wished. They argued that congregations of believers should be independent of each other and the state; electing and appointing their own ministers, elders and officers and that no institutional church should or could coerce a sincere Christian to accept or do anything against his or her conscience.

43. During Most of 1644 Both Sides Seemed Equally Matched

The year 1644 opened with the forces of the King and Parliament evenly matched and the year was to witness some spectacular successes and failures on both sides. On 19 January a Scottish army entered England, and, bypassing the Royalist garrison at Newcastle, began to march south. At the same time Waller's army was to march against Sir Ralph Hopton in southern England. In the Midlands, Rupert relieved the siege of Newark in late March and drove the Parliamentarians back into Lincolnshire, while Waller defeated Hopton on the 29th at the Battle of Cheriton. In the north, Newcastle and the Scots shadowed each other but did not come to battle until Selby fell to Fairfax on 11 April threatening York, and Newcastle fell back to defend the city. The Scots and Fairfax's forces meet at Wetherby and laid siege to York. In Oxford, the King and Rupert agreed to send forces north to relieve York.

With York threatened and the allied armies joined by Cromwell and the Eastern Association cavalry, Parliament dispatched Essex to link up with Waller in an assault upon Oxford. Essex and Waller took Reading on 19 May. Leaving Oxford well defended, the King marched west and Waller was ordered to pursue him, while Essex turned south and west, through Dorset and Devon in an attempt to defeat Hopton in the West Country. The King and Waller met in battle on 29 June at Cropredy Bridge in Oxfordshire and Waller's forces were soundly beaten.

Meanwhile Rupert's forces were approaching York and the allies raised the siege to face him. Newcastle issued forth from York to join up with Rupert. On 2 July the allied forces made up of the Scots, Yorkshire regiments under Fairfax and Eastern Association units under Manchester and Cromwell faced Rupert's and Newcastle's combined forces at Marston Moor. After an epic struggle the allied forces prevailed and the Royalists were decisively beaten. Marston Moor effectively ended the war in the north of England and the Marquess of Newcastle fled abroad. On the 16th, York surrendered to Fairfax. Decisive though the victory was, it was not adequately followed up. The Scots moved back north, while many of Fairfax's troops refused to march south out of Yorkshire. Prince Rupert had retreated back over the Pennines, but Manchester refused to pursue him.

While disaster had overtaken the Royalists in the north, in the south things were going well for the King. Having disposed of Waller at Cropredy Bridge, he pursued Essex through Devon and into Cornwall. Here the Parliamentary forces were finally cornered and defeated at Lostwithiel in late August. Essex himself escaped in a fishing boat but most of his army and equipment were captured. While the King may have lost the north, his victories at Cropredy Bridge and Lostwithiel had strengthened his position in the south-west and the south Midlands. Now let us look at these events in more detail.

44. The Scots Invaded England in 1643

After the signing of the 'Solemn League and Covenant' a Scottish force occupied Berwick-on-Tweed in September 1643, but it was not until January 1644 that the main Scottish army was ready to march into north England. This invasion immediately put the northern Royalists on the defensive as there was now every possibility that they could be caught between the Scots and the English Parliamentarians. The Scots headed for Newcastle, but the Royalists commander in the north, William Cavendish, Marquess of Newcastle, marched north from York with the main Royalist force and, with the aid of the Governor of the city, Sir Thomas Glenham, reinforced the garrison and strengthened the defences in Newcastle before the Scots arrived.

Rather than get bogged down in a long siege, the Scots bypassed Newcastle and headed for Sunderland, which declared for Parliament and opened its gates to the Scots on 4 March 1644. Taking Sunderland gave the Scots a port where supplies could be landed. Meanwhile, the Marquess of Newcastle established his headquarters at Durham and, to avoid being cut off from Royalist forces in Yorkshire, intended to establish a forward position on the River Tees at Piercebridge. But before this could be achieved, word reached Newcastle that the town of Selby had fallen to the Parliamentarians and that York, the Royalist capital in the north, was threatened.

45. The Fall of Selby, Yorkshire, Was a Disaster for the Royalists

At the same time as the Scots were marching south from Newcastle, Parliamentarian forces were harrying Royalist forces in Yorkshire. Detachments from the Parliamentarian garrison at Hull attacked Royalist positions in the East Riding, while on 3 March 1644 the Parliamentarians under Colonel John Lambert captured Bradford. With the Marquess of Newcastle still in the north the remaining Royalist forces in Yorkshire under Colonel John Belasyse were in danger of being crushed between the two wings of Parliamentarian forces. Belasyse decided to move his headquarters to Selby, an important town strategically, as it was situated between Bradford and Hull and commanded the approach to York. Reinforced by cavalry from Newark, Belasyse launched an assault upon Bradford, which came very close to success.

Having withstood the Royalist attack, Lambert was now joined in Bradford by Sir Thomas Fairfax, and on 11 April a combined Parliamentarian force of around 1,500 horse and 1,800 foot stormed Selby. After fierce fighting through the town and with Colonel Belasyse wounded and taken prisoner, the Royalists finally surrendered, most of the cavalry escaped but around 1,600 infantrymen were taken prisoner. The fall of Selby opened the way to York. Newcastle hurried south pursued by the Scots, who eventually rendezvoused with Fairfax and Lambert at Wetherby. This allied force of Scots and English Parliamentarians laid siege to York on 22 April 1644.

46. The Battle of Marston Moor Is Said to Have Been the Largest Ever Fought in England

With over 39,000 horse and foot engaged, the Battle of Marston Moor in the Vale of York on 2 July 1644 is, almost certainly, one of the largest land battles ever fought in Britain. On the Parliamentarian side it was also an alliance of disparate forces made up of the Scots under the Earl of Leven, forces of the Eastern Association under the Earl of Manchester, including Cromwell's Ironsides, and Sir Thomas Fairfax with horse and foot from Lancashire and Yorkshire. The Royalist foot were commanded by the Marquess of Newcastle, while Rupert commanded the cavalry. Numerically, the Parliamentarians had the advantage, with around 22,500 horse and foot as opposed to the 17,000 of the Royalists.

Rupert had arrived outside York the day before the battle and the York garrison marched out to meet him. Disagreements between the Royalist commanders meant they were initially taken by surprise when the Parliamentarians attacked at around 7 p.m. on the 2nd. Recovering quickly, the Royalists seemed to be getting the better of the fight; on the right flank, the Royalist cavalry broke that of the Parliamentarians and then put pressure on the infantry, which, when simultaneously attacked by the Royalist infantry, seemed to be on the verge of breaking. However, Cromwell and the Parliamentarian cavalry on the left flank had been successful and now threw themselves against Rupert's cavalry in an effort to rally the infantry, this tactic worked, and the Royalist cavalry were defeated. The Parliamentarian infantry regrouped and went over to the attack. At this point the Marquess of Newcastle's regiment of Whitecoats made a heroic last stand in an attempt to give the remaining

Royalist forces time to retreat back to York, when the Whitecoats finally surrendered there were only thirty left alive; the battle had lasted barely two hours.

The repercussions of Marston Moor were momentous: Prince Rupert, apart from losing his beloved dog, Boy, killed during the battle, finally lost his reputation for invincibility, although he did manage to gather together the remnants of the Royalist cavalry and retreat over the Pennines. York resisted a siege for a further two weeks but finally surrendered, destroying in the process Royalist military power in the north of England. The Marquess of Newcastle, ashamed at the defeat, went into exile. But all was not well with the victors. The Scots decided to move north after the battle, while Manchester declined to pursue Rupert across the Pennines. Many in the Parliamentarian camp, particularly Cromwell, were incensed by the failure of the Scots and Manchester to follow up the victory at Marston Moor and deliver a fatal blow to the Royalists. This was to give rise to a bitter quarrel over the conduct and purpose of the war among the Parliamentarians, which led to the formation of the New Model Army.

47. BRILLIANA HARLEY DEFENDED HER HOME AGAINST A ROYALIST SIEGE

It is a truism of war that women often have to take on roles traditionally reserved for men, and the Civil War was no exception. Many women found themselves in the front line, such as the women of London who helped the Trained Bands repulse the Royalists at Turnham Green in November 1642, the women who helped defend Lyme in the spring of 1644 and a number of gentry ladies who, with their husbands away fighting the war, found themselves responsible for defending their homes against the enemy. One example will suffice, that of Brilliana Harley. She was born around 1598 and married Robert Harley of Brampton Bryan, Herefordshire, in 1623. Brilliana and Robert were both Puritans and Robert, who was an MP, was closely associated with the opposition to Charles I in Parliament. Herefordshire was a predominantly Royalist county and, with Robert away in London during the spring and summer of 1642, Brilliana began to feel uneasy about the safety of herself and her children. But she obeyed her husband's instructions to stay on at Brampton Castle despite the growing hostility of her neighbours. Through the tense summer of 1642 Brilliana busied herself trying to make the castle defensible and brought in supplies of muskets, powder and shot from Hereford.

Early in 1643, Hereford was occupied by Royalist forces and life at Brampton deteriorated, Brilliana found it impossible to collect her rents, she complained to her husband that their tenants had grown rude and insubordinate and that she and her staff and servants were afraid to venture far from the castle. In early February she heard that the Royalist Sheriff of Radnorshire had been instructed to lead a force against Brampton, to capture and destroy it. Brilliana was saved on this occasion by the fact that the sheriff's men refused to cross the border into England and the Hereford Royalists were ordered away to attack Gloucester. But Brampton remained effectively under siege and the Governor of Hereford gave her the choice of surrendering or face an attack. This time Brilliana was saved by the advent of a Parliamentarian army under Sir William Waller in which two of her sons were serving. But the Parliamentarian defeat at the Battle of Roundway Down in Wiltshire tilted the advantage in Herefordshire once more in the direction of the Royalists. On 26 July 1643, the event Brilliana had dreaded for over a year finally took place when two to three troops of horse and 200–300 foot appeared before Brampton Castle and Brilliana was ordered to surrender – she refused. Inside the castle were Brilliana, her three youngest children, about fifty musketeers and their officer as well as servants and other tenants and civilians who had taken refuge in the castle.

By the beginning of August the siege was tightening. The Royalists burnt the village, took away all the cattle and sheep on the estate and brought up cannon, one of which they mounted on the roof of Brampton Bryan Church from which to bombard the castle. Despite the siege and the bombardment the garrison held on until, on 23 August, a messenger arrived from the King calling on Brilliana to surrender; again she refused, and managed to spin out the negotiations until early September when she learnt that a large Parliamentarian army was marching to the relief of Gloucester. This meant that the siege was soon lifted and the Royalist forces were ordered to help counter the threat of this new Parliamentarian army to the south. Brilliana now went on the offensive, sending out a small party to attack a Royalist troop in nearby Knighton.

On 9 October she wrote to her eldest son, Ned, complaining of a severe cold. Perhaps it was a result of the months of stress and anxiety, but the cold soon developed into something much worse, until her health had completely collapsed and she died on 31 October. The broken-hearted garrison remained in possession of the castle until the spring of 1644. In March the Royalists returned once more before its gates, the garrison held out for three weeks before finally surrendering on 3 April.

48. In the South-West, Charles Defeated the Earl of Essex

Bristol fell to the Royalists in July 1643 and, led initially by the Earl of Carnarvon and then by Prince Maurice, they consolidated their hold on the south-west, taking Dorchester, Weymouth, Portland, Exeter and Dartmouth. Maurice also besieged Plymouth but strong resistance forced the Royalists to abandon the siege in late December. In April 1644, Maurice besieged the Parliamentarian port of Lyme in Dorset, which held out for two months. With the approach of the Earl of Essex, Maurice was obliged to raise the siege and withdraw to Exeter. Essex followed him into Devon, bypassed Exeter and made for Plymouth from where, with the aid of the Earl of Warwick's Parliamentarian navy, he hoped to break Royalist power in the south-west.

Essex was assured that Cornwall was eager to rise up against the Royalists and change sides, and so, on 26 July, Essex, with an army of over 10,000, crossed into Cornwall and arrived at Bodmin. Unfortunately for him, the hoped-for Cornish rebellion did not materialise. Not only that, but he soon learnt that a Royalist force over 15,000 strong, led by the King and Maurice, were hot on his heels. Essex withdrew to the port of Lostwithiel, hoping to be rescued by Warwick and the fleet. He was now trapped in Lostwithiel and contrary winds made it impossible for Warwick to sail up the River Fowey. On 31 August the Parliamentarian cavalry succeeded in breaking through Royalist lines but the foot was in a desperate situation. The following day Essex slipped down the Fowey Estuary in a fishing boat and out to sea, and on 2 September his abandoned army surrendered to the King.

49. THE NEW MODEL ARMY WON THE WAR FOR PARLIAMENT

The King's success in the Midlands and the south-west, together with the failure to follow up the victory at Marston Moor, convinced many in the Parliamentary 'war party' that there was something profoundly wrong with their commanders. These frustrations and enmities emerged in November 1644 when Cromwell presented his complaints concerning Manchester's leadership of the army of the Eastern Association to the House of Commons. The controversy was not just about strategy and tactics, it reflected deep divisions within the Parliamentary camp about the way the war was being fought and how it should be prosecuted. It also reflected divisions between the Lords and the Commons and between Presbyterians and Independents.

In December, after fierce and often acrimonious debate, it was proposed to radically reorganise the army and, in an attempt to make it more professional, it was put forward that no member of the Lords or Commons should hold any military or naval command. This proposal passed the Commons on 19 December but it was not until April 1645 that the Lords finally passed what became known as the 'Self-Denying Ordinance'. By this ordinance the earls of Essex and Manchester lost their command of the armies of Parliament while the Earl of Warwick lost his command of the navy. What the Self-Denying Ordinance created was a 'New Model Army', which, although based largely on the army of the Eastern Association, was to be a unified, national force under the command of Sir Thomas Fairfax. The following month, Cromwell and Sir Arthur Brereton were exempt from the provisions of the ordinance, and Cromwell, although still an MP, was appointed Lieutenant-General of Horse and second in command to Fairfax in the new force. It was this New Model Army that was to win the war for Parliament and provide the means for Cromwell's eventual rise to power.

50. The Battle of Naseby Destroyed the King's Field Army

The campaigning season of 1645 opened with the Royalists doing well in the Midlands and south-west, while Parliament was victorious in the north and east. Parliament initially ordered Fairfax to march to relieve the siege of Taunton, but in May 1645 he was ordered to march on Oxford instead. The King and Rupert, meanwhile, were marching north but on hearing that Oxford was threatened, Charles turned back, taking and sacking Leicester on 30–31 May. Parliament then ordered Fairfax to raise the siege of Oxford and march north to intercept the King.

The two armies met near the village of Naseby, just south of Market Harborough, on the Leicestershire/Northamptonshire border on 14 June. The Royalists, commanded by the King, Prince Rupert and the Sergeant-Major-General of Foot, Lord Astley, consisted of 4–5,000 foot and between 3,500 and 5,000 horse, while the New Model, commanded by Sir Thomas Fairfax, Cromwell and Philip Skippon as Sergeant-Major-General of Foot, comprised around 7,000 foot, 5,500–6,000 horse, 1,000 dragoons and 11 cannon. Although outnumbered, to begin with the Royalists gained the advantage when Rupert's cavalry broke through their opponents on the Parliamentarian left flank. But instead of turning about to engage the Parliamentarian foot in the centre they followed their usual routine of riding off the battlefield to attack the baggage train. Meanwhile the Royalist infantry advanced and, to begin with, seemed about to overwhelm the Parliamentarian infantry. But Fairfax intervened to help stop a rout and the remaining cavalry from the Parliamentarian left flank regrouped and attacked the flank of the Royalist infantry, now the superiority of numbers began to tell in the Parliamentarian's favour.

On the Parliamentarian right flank, Cromwell charged against the Royalist Northern Horse led by Sir Marmaduke Langdale. After fierce fighting Cromwell's force slowly began to push the Royalists back. Cromwell also sent some of his cavalry to attack the Royalist infantry in the centre of the battlefield and, beset on three sides, the Royalist infantry began to fall back. The final phase of the battle consisted of a final stand by Rupert's regiment of Bluecoats, but again, the Bluecoats became surrounded and were cut to pieces.

It was at this point that Rupert and his men arrived back on the battlefield, but they were too late to turn the tide and could only help cover the Royalist retreat. Watching the debacle from a nearby hill, Charles wanted to lead a last, gallant, charge into the thick of the battle with his Lifeguards; this would have almost certainly resulted in either his capture or death. It is said that the Earl of Carnwath riding next to the King, seized the bridle of his horse, told him in no uncertain terms what a stupid thing it would be and pulled him aside. The remains of the Royalist right wing made a last stand at a place called Wadborough Hill, around 2 miles north of the main battlefield, but the majority of the Royalist army were pursued and slaughtered along the road back to Leicester.

One particularly nasty incident occurred when the New Model overran the Royalist baggage train. They found lots of women speaking a strange language that the soldiers assumed was Irish. To the Parliamentarians, Irish equalled Papist and, if women, that meant they were whores. They therefore inflicted the penalty meted out to prostitutes in the seventeenth century; they mutilated them, slashing their faces with their daggers and slitting their noses – many women were killed. But the women were neither Irish nor whores, instead they were the wives and daughters of the men fighting in the King's army and the strange language they were speaking was Welsh.

However, the New Model Army had proved its worth in battle, the Royalist field army was effectively cut to pieces at Naseby and most of the King's artillery and supplies were captured. Charles retired to Hereford and hoped that a new field army could be raised from fresh recruits in Wales. Yet with money running low how was he to pay this new army? Rupert took command of Bristol, with a plan to bring over an army from Ireland. In August, Fairfax and Cromwell arrived before Bristol and laid siege to the city, while Charles, frustrated in his attempts to raise an effective army in south Wales, moved north with the intention of linking up with Royalist forces in Scotland. Encountering stiff resistance in Yorkshire, Charles fell back on Newark and on the 28th arrived back in Oxford. On 10 September Bristol fell to the New Model.

Without a field army to come to their aid, Royalist garrison, although numerous, were isolated and vulnerable. Throughout the remainder of 1645 and into 1646 they were picked off one by one by the New Model. Having defeated the Royalists in the south-west and taken Bristol, Fairfax returned to besieging Oxford. Charles left the city in disguise on 27 April and the Royalist capital finally surrendered on 24 June, just over a year since the Battle of Naseby. A few Royalist garrisons still held out, but, with the surrender of Oxford, the Civil War was effectively over. Having won the war, Parliament now had to win the peace.

51. Now All Parliament Had To Do Was Win the Peace!

If Parliament thought winning the war was difficult, it was nothing compared to the complexity of the negotiations that attempted to settle the nation, and one of the greatest difficulties Parliament was to face was the King himself. After slipping out of besieged Oxford in disguise on 27 April 1646, Charles finally surrendered to the Scots at Southwell in Nottinghamshire on 5 May. The siege of Oxford dragged on for another six weeks, the garrison finally surrendering to Fairfax on 24 June. With the fall of Oxford the first Civil War came to an end. Now was the time for the victorious Parliament and its Scottish allies to settle the issues that had led the country into civil war, but, as I have said, the search for settlement proved to be long and complicated. There were two reasons for this: the first was that no one in 1646 believed that a lasting settlement could be achieved without the agreement of the King. Charles knew this and tried to play a divide-and-rule game with his enemies in the hope that if the wartime alliance broke apart he might, somehow, be able to recover his throne on his own terms. The second reason why the search for settlement proved so difficult was because the members of the wartime alliance – the English Parliament, the Scots and the New Model Army – all had different agendas and a different vision of what post-war England should look like. The Scots and their English Presbyterian allies wanted to establish the Presbyterian system in England, but very soon disputes arose between the Scots and the English Presbyterians over control of the Church by Parliament and the New Model was implacably opposed to the introduction of a coercive and exclusive Presbyterian system, which, they argued, was as bad as Laud's Anglican Church against which they had just fought. These divisions among the allies frustrated the search for settlement and encouraged Charles to believe that his wait-and-see and divide-and-rule strategies would eventually see his enemies fighting each other and would, in turn, provide an opportunity for him to regain his throne on his own terms.

52. THE WESTMINSTER ASSEMBLY ATTEMPTED TO REFORM THE ENGLISH CHURCH

Back in November 1641 the Grand Remonstrance recommended that a church synod or assembly be convened to reform the Church of England along more 'godly' lines. Following a Parliamentary ordinance the Assembly first met at Westminster Abbey on 1 July 1643. The Assembly consisted of 120 clergymen and theologians chosen from each English and Welsh County, together with ten members of the Lords and thirty MPs. As Parliament was in the process of negotiating a treaty with the Presbyterian Scots, twelve Scottish commissioners also attended the Assembly.

The 'Solemn League and Covenant' gave the Presbyterians the upper hand in the Assembly and plans were discussed not only to introduce the Presbyterian Church system into England and Wales, but also to join the English and Scottish churches in a formal union. However, there was a vociferous minority of Independents who rejected any idea of a universal, coercive, Presbyterian system in England and they were joined by a third group, who were called 'the Erastians', who argued that, unlike Scotland, the English Church should be firmly under the control of Parliament.

Although the Assembly produced *The Directory of Public Worship* to take the place of the *Book of Common Prayer*, which was formally banned in January 1645, a *Confession of Faith*, two *Catechisms*, and *The Form of Presbyterial Church-Government*, the aim to remodel the Church of England along Presbyterian lines failed. This was due principally to the dogged adherence of the King and the Royalists to episcopal Anglicanism and the *Book of Common Prayer*, and the strength of the Independents in the army.

53. THE NEW MODEL ARMY PROVOKED A GREAT OUTBURST OF POLITICAL RADICALISM

The Civil War brought death and disruption to many people, but it also provoked a questioning of many of the assumptions upon which society was based. The authority of the King was being challenged on the battlefield, the structures and liturgy of the Church of England were under sustained attack by Puritans and radical religious sects proliferated. The familiar rhythms and rituals of the year was also under attack, even the subordinate position of women was being questioned. Some greeted this upheaval and questioning with enthusiasm while many others regarded it as a great threat to the established, divinely ordained, structures and norms of society.

Since its inception the New Model possessed a distinct character based, initially, on Cromwell's determination that it should be recruited as far as possible from the ranks of 'well affected' Independents. Having fought side by side in 1645 and 1646 and been victorious the officers and men soon found they had a common cause in resisting Parliamentary attempts to disband them. It was this sense of a common identity and common grievances that gave the New Model a voice in English politics, first at Saffron Walden in March 1647 and later the same year at Putney in October and November. The soldiers' grievances and sense of purpose coincided with the radical political programmes being put forward by the Levellers in 1647. Leveller leaders and writers such as John Lilburne, Richard Overton, William Walwyn and John Wildman shared the same Independent religious background of the officers and men of the New Model. Many of them, including Lilburne, had served in Parliamentarian armies and Wildman was a New Model soldier and an agitator at Putney. They shared the hopes and the religious convictions of the soldiers and they could articulate the emerging political demands of the army. At the same time the political power of the army gave a platform and a significance to Leveller ideas far beyond anything the leaders of the movement could have achieved alone. The unity between religious and political radicalism in this period is summed up in the motto on one regimental standard, which read: 'No King but King Jesus'.

54. Cromwell Believed in Religious Toleration

We have seen that the logic of the Independent position regarding the institutional church made them tolerate a wide variety of religious groups. No one was more aware of the importance of this need for toleration than Cromwell. Speaking of different types of government, Cromwell said that they were all, 'dross and dung compared to Christ'.* In other words, he was largely indifferent to the forms of government as long as godliness was encouraged and prospered in the individual and society. If true godliness flourished, good government, whatever its form, would result. Likewise, he felt the same about the finer details of different doctrines and Church structures, he was largely indifferent to the labels different sects applied to themselves – Baptist, Independent, Fifth Monarchist, etc. – as long as individuals were Bible-based Protestants and worked to know and obey God's will then the label they might attach to themselves was a thing indifferent. Cromwell also believed that to silence a godly person was a serious matter, as that person might have 'a word from the Lord' to impart to the community of the faithful. Such attitudes explain Cromwell's tolerant attitude to different religious groups and his reluctance to persecute those who differed from him over religion.

In this Cromwell was unusual for his age. The accepted attitude of both Roman Catholics and most Protestants was that there could be only one truth; if your church taught and upheld the truth, any individual or group who differed from you must, by definition, be wrong, in error and heretical. It was the duty of the Church authorities to teach the truth, guard against error and punish those who wilfully persisted in error. It was also widely believed that it was impossible for two religious 'truths' to exist simultaneously in the same state, the result would be conflict and anarchy. But Cromwell and, increasingly, the Independent congregations, argued that truth was found by the individual Christian seeking God and God's mercy to the individual believer could not be confined within restrictive and exclusive Church structures.

*Brailsford, H. N., *The Levellers and the English Revolution*. (Stanford, Cal.: Stanford University Press, 1961), p. 286. Cromwell is paraphrasing St Paul, Philippians 3:8.

55. THE NEW MODEL ARMY PROPOSED RELIGIOUS TOLERATION

In 1647, the army presented its own peace treaty to the King and the 'Heads of the Proposals', as this document was called, not only provided the basis for a comprehensive peace independent of Parliament, it was also the first occasion when a broad toleration for different Protestant sects was officially put forward. Article 11 proposed the abolition of 'all coercive power, authority, and jurisdiction of bishops and other ecclesiastical officers'. Article 12 demanded the repeal of the Uniformity Acts, which had been passed under Elizabeth, James and Charles and which established the Church of England and the *Book of Common Prayer* as the sole legal expression of public religion in England. They also demanded the abolition of all laws forcing everyone to attend their local parish church each Sunday on pain of punishment. Article 13 also demanded that the taking of the Presbyterian Covenant be declared invalid if forced on anyone 'against their judgments or consciences'.* What the army was proposing was the systematic dismantling of coercive church structures and that liberty of conscience in matters of religious belief and practice should, for the first time in England and with certain exceptions, be guaranteed by law.

*Gardiner, S. R., *The Constitutional Documents of the Puritan Revolution 1625–1660*, 3rd edition (Oxford: Clarendon Press, 1906), p. 321.

56. Fifth Monarchists and Prophets Preached the Coming of 'King Jesus'

We have seen how Puritanism insisted upon the duty of each Christian to find God through their own efforts aided solely by the Bible. We have also seen how the Independents believed in a wide toleration for different religious views. When these two beliefs were combined, it produced during the 1640s an outpouring of religious groups, sects and cults all claiming a unique call from God and all basing their particular beliefs and practices upon some text of the Bible. Chief among these were the various Baptist congregations who rejected the institutional church and infant baptism. Adult Baptism – or 'dipping' as it was called – was reserved for those who had undergone a true conversion experience. Dipping was usually done in a river or lake where the candidate was immersed fully in the water, symbolizing the death of their old unredeemed life and their rising to a new, Christian life.

It was also a time when many came to believe that the downfall of the King and the bishops demonstrated that the end of the world was imminent and that Jesus would soon appear to reign in person. The Fifth Monarchy movement, in particular, preached the need for repentance and struggle against the reprobate to prepare the earth for the reign of Jesus; while the Ranters claimed that they had the spirit of God within them and, as that spirit could do no wrong, they could behave as they pleased and were released from all man-made laws and moral conventions. Prophets also appeared, claiming to have a special message from God, or even, in some cases, that they were the second coming. These prophets gathered followers around them. Many of them came and went very quickly, some, like the Muggletonians, followers of a prophet called Lodowick Muggleton, survived after the end of the Civil War. Another group that flourished in the 1650 were the Quakers, inspired by the preaching and writing of George Fox. They, too, claimed to have 'the light within', which guided them into truth. The early Quakers were often violent in confronting conventional religion and attracted many who had passed through other congregations and sects.

The rise of this startling array of radical congregations, sects, prophets and downright lunatics caused alarm and fear among the more conservative members of society. They were accustomed to order and uniformity in religion, and a church dominated by the gentry and the university educated clergy. These radical groups, which seemed to spring up from nowhere and often claimed a spiritual authority that defied the magistrate and the state, were viewed as dangerous, subversive, heretical and symptomatic of a society in crisis and of a 'world turned upside down'.

57. MATTHEW HOPKINS HUNTED WITCHES IN EAST ANGLIA

We considered earlier how important to Puritans was the concept of 'spiritual warfare', how the Christian life was a continual struggle against the Devil and the forces of darkness. This conviction probably lies behind the activities of Matthew Hopkins in East Anglia between 1645 and 1647 when he provoked a witch-craze during which many innocent people died. We know virtually nothing about his early life apart from the fact that he was the son of James Hopkins, vicar of Wenham in Suffolk and was born sometime between 1615 and 1620. Whatever his motives and reasons, in the winter of 1644–45, Hopkins, who was living in the village of Manningtree, Essex, suddenly began to accuse a number of village women of being witches, of having made a pact with the Devil and of harming their neighbours through diabolic means. Eventually, in July 1645, thirty-six suspects were tried before the Essex Assizes and nineteen were hung as witches. A further nine women had died in prison while awaiting trial and six more were still languishing in prison in 1648. One woman was acquitted, while another saved herself by giving evidence for the prosecution. From Essex the witch-craze, spurred on by Hopkins and his associate John Stearne, spread across East Anglia. It has been estimated that around 250 people, mainly women, were accused and examined for witchcraft, of whom around a hundred were hanged, while many more died in prison.

Why did a witch-craze on this scale erupt in this place and at this time? East Anglia was part of the Puritan heartland, dominated by radical Puritan ministers and gentry who would have been aware of the presence and dangers of witches. When this is combined with the anxiety and stress caused by the war, the absence of husbands, fathers, brothers, etc., in the army and a general war-weariness caused by the ongoing crisis in the country, we have, perhaps, the conditions where men like Hopkins and Stearne could provoke hysteria against a supposed hidden enemy. We must also take into account their methods in obtaining confessions; the accused were stripped and their bodies searched for the 'Devil's mark' – to spot where their imp or familiar sucked their blood. They were also 'watched' by Hopkins and his assistants to see if their familiar returned to them. In practice, this was a form of sleep depredation that soon broke down the resistance of the accused and which usually not only produced a detailed confession but also the accusation of others who were then arrested and subject to the same treatment. The witch-craze ended as abruptly as it had begun, with the death of Hopkins in August 1647.

58. John Lilburne Was One of the Leaders of the Levellers

In Fact 53 we met John Lilburne and the Levellers and it is now time to say more about them. Lilburne (1616–57) was the most famous of the Leveller leaders and a prolific pamphleteer in which he denounced the power of the ruling elites and called for the radical reform of the political and economic system. Born the second son of a Durham gentry family, he was the author of over eighty pamphlets and petitions and suffered imprisonment seven times for his views. In 1630, he was apprenticed to a wholesale clothier in London and soon became involved in separatist Calvinist congregations. In 1637, he was tried before Star Chamber for writing against the bishops and was flogged through the streets of London, pilloried and imprisoned. He was not released until 1640 on the petitioning of Cromwell in the Long Parliament. On his release he joined a Parliamentary regiment; captured by the Royalists, he was imprisoned in Oxford between November 1642 and May 1643. After release by the Royalists he fought again for Parliament, rising to the rank of Lieutenant-Colonel, but resigned his commission rather than take the Presbyterian covenant in 1644. Imprisoned again by Parliament for his attacks on the Earl of Manchester, he nevertheless cultivated many contacts with radical religious and political groups and individuals in London and was in a position to exploit the growing radicalism and discontent in the New Model Army in 1646 and 1647. With William Walwyn, Richard Overton and John Wildman, Lilburne articulated Leveller demands for a more equitable franchise and religious toleration.

The Leveller movement was never a disciplined political party in the modern sense with a defined and agreed manifesto. Rather it was an alliance of radical voices putting forward different ideas and concerns. Some Levellers concentrated on the religious question and campaigned for toleration, others campaigned to reform the franchise and Parliament. Levellers disagreed over who should have the vote: should all men have the vote, did women have political rights? Should there be a property qualification and if so, what should it be? Should domestic servants be given the vote? Should Catholics be included within the scope of religious toleration? Should the king be retained as a figurehead or should England become a republic? These and similar questions were vigorously discussed and debated. But what all Levellers had in common was a vision of post-war England that was democratic and egalitarian, where the representatives of the people should be directly accountable to the people and where a broad religious toleration was guaranteed by law.

As for Lilburne, as the Leveller movement declined after 1649 he was tried for treason by the new Commonwealth but acquitted amid scenes of popular rejoicing, for Lilburne was always very popular among the ordinary people of London. In 1652, he was again tried and exiled for libel and on his unauthorised return to England in 1653 he was again tried for treason and again acquitted among yet more scenes of popular rejoicing. Despite the acquittal, Cromwell exiled him to Jersey and, from 1655, imprisoned him without trial in Dover Castle. In his later years Lilburne was influenced by the writings of George Fox and died a Quaker. The writings of Lilburne and the Levellers, rediscovered at the end of the nineteenth century, influenced some British socialist thinkers and historians in the twentieth century.

59. The Leveller Richard Overton Argued For Inherent Natural Rights

We know nothing about Richard Overton's early life – where or when he was born, etc. – the first time he enters the historical record is between 1640 and 1642 when he published a series of attacks on Laud and his church reforms. In 1645 he attacked the Presbyterians, denouncing them as being every bit as tyrannical and violent in their attitudes as the Laudians in the 1630s. These attacks on the Presbyterians proved popular with the Independents and the army and Overton moved on to write on political issues such as reform of the law, the abolition of tithes, the excise tax and monopolies; he also called for annual Parliaments, demands which were to become fundamental to the Leveller movement. In July 1646 *The Remonstrance of Many Thousand Citizens* appeared, which was probably written by Overton and William Walwyn and is seen as an important statement of Leveller ideas.

Meanwhile, John Lilburne had been imprisoned in the Tower on the orders of the House of Lords for denouncing the Earl of Manchester as a secret Royalist, and Overton wrote in support of the campaign to get Lilburne released. When he accused the Lords of being an arbitrary power similar to the King he was himself arrested and committed to Newgate Prison. It was while in prison that Overton wrote *An Arrow Against all Tyrants and Tyrany* (sic), the opening paragraph of which contains one of the first defences of the idea of inherent natural rights. All men, writes Overton, are born with certain fundamental rights of self-government, freedom and liberty. These rights are inherent in the fact of our birth and humanity, they are not granted by any external power and to invade the rights of an individual is to perform an act of tyranny; as he says, 'No man has power over my rights and liberties, and I over no man's.' This language of inherent natural rights was later to form the basis of the political philosophy of liberalism; it was to surface again in the work of John Locke at the end of the seventeenth century and was to resound through the political theory of both the American and French Revolutions in the eighteenth century.

Here is the passage in full:

> To every individual in nature is given an individual property by nature not to be invaded or usurped in any. For every one, as he is himself, so he hath a self-propriety, else could he not be himself; and of this no second may presume to deprive any of without manifest violation and affront to the very principles of nature and of the rules of equity and justice between man and man. Mine and thine cannot be, except this be. No man has power over my rights and liberties, and I over no man's. I may be but an individual, enjoy myself and my self-propriety and may right myself no more than myself, or presume any further; if I do, I am an encroacher and an invader upon another man's right – to which I have no right. For by natural birth all men are equally and alike born to like propriety, liberty and freedom; and as we are delivered of God by the hand of nature into this world, every one with a natural, innate freedom and propriety (as it were writ in the table of every man's heart, never to be obliterated) even so are we to live, everyone equally and alike to enjoy his birthright and privilege; even all thereof God by nature has made him free.*

(NB: 'Propriety' is a seventeenth-century spelling for 'property'.)

*Richard Overton, *An arrow against all tyrants and tyrany (sic) shot from the prison of New-gate into the prerogative bowels of the arbitrary House of Lords, and all other usurpers and tyrants whatsoever.* London, 12 October 1646.

60. LEVELLER WOMEN DEMANDED THE VOTE

Although the Levellers were not a political party in the modern sense, they did have some features that resembled a modern political party such as committees, subscriptions, petitions, party colours (sea green) and a newspaper, etc., but they did not fight elections or produce a detailed manifesto of policies. Rather they were a pressure group, trying to influence the opinions and policies of those with power in the army and Parliament. The leading writers often took different views on major questions, one of the most important of them being who should have the right to vote? Colonel Rainsborough at Putney famously declared the 'the poorest he that is in England has a right to live as the greatest he', and that no one should be obliged to live under a government he had not had the opportunity to vote for.* But was Rainsborough advocating universal suffrage? He talks of 'he', did he just envision men having the vote? Other Levellers sought to deny the vote to women and apprentices on the grounds that without a secret ballot these groups were not independent and could be influenced to vote the way their husbands and masters wished. Others argued that Royalists and Catholics should be excluded as they constituted a threat to the state.

One group of people decided to take matters into their own hands and in May 1649 a group of Leveller women presented a petition to Parliament demanding the vote. This was in the aftermath of the revolutionary events of December 1648 to January 1649 – the purge of Parliament by the army and the trial and execution of the King. Many radicals hoped that these momentous events heralded the beginning of revolution – they were to be disappointed.

The argument put forward by the women was based upon the fact that they were, like men, created in the image of God and that they should share with men in the freedoms and privileges guaranteed by the Commonwealth. Women, they went on, had also shared in the hardships and sacrifices of the war that, they argued, had brought the King to justice and overthrown tyranny and on this basis they had the same right as men to petition. This petition is a remarkable document and appears to be the first time in England that women had gathered together and publically voiced their demand to be considered equal to men. The response of the sober, godly, gentlemen in Parliament can be predicted. They rebuked the women for wasting their time and reminded them that they had already discussed this question with their husbands. The MPs considered that the women would be better employed returning to their homes and their husbands and attending to what they called their 'housewifery'.

* Wootton, D. *Divine Right and Democracy: An Anthology of Political Writing in Stuart England* (Harmondsworth: Penguin Books, 1986), p. 286.

61. Many Ideas of the Levellers Were Only Implemented Hundreds of Years Later

To our eyes much of the Levellers' agenda seems very sensible. However much of it appears to have just disappeared off the map after the Restoration. I thought it was worth looking at some of the main Leveller demands to see what became of them – it makes some interesting reading!

1. The right to vote for those over the age of twenty-one (excepting servants, apprentices, beggars and Royalists and, after some debate, women).
Universal male suffrage for those over twenty-one finally arrived in the UK in 1918, although the vast majority of men had been enfranchised with the passage of the Third Reform Act of 1884. Women over thirty-one who were ratepayers, or married to a ratepayer, were also given the vote in 1918. This was amended in 1928 so that all women over twenty-one could vote. The voting age was lowered to eighteen in 1969 and during the Scottish referendum in 2015 the voting age was lowered to sixteen. (The secret ballot was introduced in 1872.)

2. The equalization of Parliamentary constituencies to ensure that communities were fairly represented.
Rotten Boroughs (as they became known) were not abolished until the Reform Act of 1832. Today constituency boundaries are periodically reviewed to take account of population changes.

3. Abolition of the House of Lords.
Still being debated – no sign of abolition.

4. No army officer, treasurer or lawyer could be an MP (to prevent conflict of interest).
Armed Forces Officers are now excluded as are judges and civil servants (which might equate loosely to treasurer) the House of Commons is stuffed with lawyers!

5. Annual elections to Parliament with MPs not being allowed to serve consecutive terms.
The Meeting of Parliament Act 1694 fixed the maximum term to three years – subsequently changed to seven years in 1716 and to five years in 1911. MPs can serve as often as they can be re-elected

6. Freedom of worship (which, after some debate, continued to exclude Catholics).
The Toleration Act of 1689 gave Nonconformists limited toleration. However, they could not stand for public office unless they were willing to take communion in the Church of England at least once a year and all but Anglicans were excluded from Oxford and Cambridge Universities until 1871.

The Catholic Relief Act of 1791 gave Catholics freedom to worship. It also removed a wide range of other restrictions and allowed Catholics their own schools, to hold junior public offices, and to live in London. They were allowed to become MPs after the passage of the Catholic Emancipation Act in 1829.

In 1861, after almost thirty years of campaigning, Jews were allowed to take their seats in Parliament without having to swear an oath to uphold the Christian religion.

In 1888 the Oaths Act, sponsored by Charles Bradlaugh, made it possible for atheists to take a revised form of the oath necessary to take their seat in Parliament. Today, two versions of the oath are available to MPs as a result of the Oaths Act 1978: 'I ... swear by Almighty God that I will be faithful and bear true allegiance to Her Majesty Queen Elizabeth, her heirs and successors, according to law. So help me God.' Or: 'I ... do solemnly, sincerely and truly declare and affirm that I will be faithful and bear true allegiance to Her Majesty Queen Elizabeth, her heirs and successors, according to law.'

7. Disestablishment of the Church of England.

In 1662, the Church of England was re-established (if I can put it like that) as the one, lawful, expression of religion in England.

The Church of Ireland was disestablished in 1871 and the Church of Wales was disestablished in 1920.

The position of the Presbyterian Church of Scotland is more complicated. It is recognised as 'the national church' and the monarch takes an oath 'to maintain and preserve the Protestant religion and Presbyterian Church government'. But no Scots Presbyterians have reserved places in Parliament either in Westminster or Edinburgh.

The position today is that twenty-six Anglican bishops sit in the Lords – this includes the archbishops of York and Canterbury. The monarch is the Supreme Governor of the Church of England and the Church is a major landowner and the English school system is still dominated by the Church of England. Since the Succession to the Crown Act of 2013, marrying a Roman Catholic does not bar one from the succession. However, under the 1701 Act of Settlement the monarch must be 'in communion with the Church of England', although the present situation is ambiguous: the 2013 act assumes that the monarch will be a member of the Church of England, even if married to a Catholic or a person of any other Christian denomination, or faith, or of no faith, while the Church of England remains established and the monarch remains Supreme Governor.

Most of the older colleges in Oxford and Cambridge retain an Anglican dean or chaplain and non-Anglican or non-Christian chaplains in hospitals and prisons, etc., are admitted at the discretion of the Anglican post holder.

8. Equality of all persons before the law including such reforms as trial (by independently selected) jury, the use of English in court, ability to refuse to incriminate oneself, and a six-month limit on the length of trials.
Use of English for all court proceedings and documents was enacted by the Rump Parliament in November 1650. The independence of the jury from the judge was established in (Bushell's Case) 1670. Significantly, the right to remain silent has recently been challenged, although I'm not sure what the current state of play is.

9. The death penalty to be applied only in cases of murder.
In 1810, there were still 220 crimes that were punishable by death. In 1861 this was reduced to five, which remained in force until capital punishment was abolished in the UK in 1965. Northern Ireland abolished the death penalty in 1973.

10. Abolition of imprisonment for debt.
The Debtors Act 1869 removed most cases of imprisonment for debt (and debtors prisons), although it is still possible to be imprisoned for debt today.

11. Tithes should be abolished and parishioners have the right to choose their ministers.
Tithes were actually not fully abolished until the Finance Act 1977. In most Nonconformist churches the minister is appointed by the congregation. In the Church of

England ministers are appointed by the diocesan bishop. (I'm not sure what happens in the Church of Scotland.)

12. Abolition of military conscription, monopolies and excise taxes.

Conscription was not a feature of army or naval recruitment in Britain until the First Word War and the Second World War, despite the press gang!

Conscription was introduced in the UK in 1916 and abolished in 1920. It was reintroduced in 1939 on the eve of the Second World War.

In 1947, conscription – called National Service - was reintroduced; initially for eighteen months, later for two years. It was abolished in 1960, the last National Serviceman leaving the British armed forces in 1963. The only exception today (2015) in the British Armed Forces is the Royal Bermuda Regiment, which is recruited through a draft lottery of Bermudan men aged between eighteen and twenty-three.

European countries that retain some element of National Service include Austria, Cyprus, Estonia, Finland, Greece, Lithuania (reintroduced in 2015), Russia, Switzerland and Ukraine.

The Bill of Rights 1689 abolished the monarch's power to enact laws and to award monopolies.

Excise Duty is, unfortunately, still very much with us!

62. Gerrard Winstanley and the Diggers Wanted to Abolish Private Property

Very little is known about Winstanley's early life, but it is believed that he was born in Wigan and that his father was a mercer. It is also apparent that he received a good education at some point as his writings are eloquent and sophisticated. In 1630, at around the age of twenty, Winstanley was apprenticed in London to Sarah Gater of the Merchant Taylors' Company and lived in the parish of St Michael, Cornhill. In 1638, Winstanley was accepted into the Merchant Taylors' Guild and he settled in the parish of St Olave, Old Jewry, as a householder and shopkeeper in the retail cloth trade. The following year he married Susan King.

Under the impact of the Civil War, the cloth trade went into decline and Winstanley was declared bankrupt at the end of 1643. He moved to Cobham, Surrey, to be near his wife's family. With the help of the Kings, Winstanley seems to have become a grazier, preparing stock for sale at market, but by 1647 a combination of high taxation and bad harvests had ruined Winstanley again. It was during this period of frustration and uncertainty that Winstanley seems to have experienced some sort of conversion, as a result of which he began to articulate his ideal of rural communist communities.

We know little of Winstanley's religious allegiance before the mid-1640s, but he seems to have been associated with certain independent congregations and refers to 'having gone through the ordinance of dipping', which means he was baptised into a Baptist congregation. Also, his companion in the Digger movement, William Everard, had been a soldier in the Parliamentarian army, a radical and a member of independent congregations.

Between 1649 and 1651, a series of communities emerged based on Winstanley's ideas. They held all property in common and sought to cultivate common land for the good of all. Winstanley called his movement the 'True Levellers', but they very soon became known as 'Diggers' as digging up common and waste ground became symbolic of transforming the earth into a 'common treasury for all'. Winstanley, in a series of pamphlets, articulated his philosophy of rural communism, which argued that misery, fear, poverty and hunger were caused by private property and private greed; these problems would be solved if all property were held in common and the 'stinking waters of self-interest' restrained. Winstanley also suggested that when true communism was achieved man would somehow return to the peace and happiness of the Garden of Eden.

Despite Winstanley's persuasive prose, all the Digger communities failed, and after associating with certain independent congregations Winstanley seems to have returned to live with his wife's family in Surrey, where he eventually acquired some land. After the Restoration, Winstanley appears in the records as a parish officer in Cobham and Elmbridge, which suggests that he conformed to the restored Church of England. In 1664, he married Elizabeth Stanley by whom he had three children. He died in 1676 and was buried in a Quaker burial ground in Westminster.

Although on a practical level the Digger movement was short-lived and a failure, Winstanley's writings remain as one of the most radical proposals for the reordering of society to emerge from the turmoil of the 1640s and, like the Levellers, his vision of rural communist communities influenced some socialist thinkers in the twentieth century.

63. ALL THE RADICAL MOVEMENTS EVENTUALLY FAILED

It is difficult to assess the extent of support for radical political movements such as the Levellers and Diggers in the late 1640s. As we have seen, some people were no doubt enthused by the 'time of shaking' to hope that a new millennium was about to usher in a time of peace and social justice when the saints would rule. Others viewed the 'time of shaking' with fear and apprehension as all the accepted structures and hierarchies in state, church and society either collapsed or were called into question. What is certain is that none of the reforms of either the Levellers or the Diggers were put into practice at the time. They were all to be defeated by vested interests and a conservatism that, by the late 1640s, wanted an end to 'shaking', disruption and high taxation and a return to peace, normality and the 'good old laws' in church and state. What is also noticeable about such figures as Lilburne and Winstanley is that with the failure of their social and political ambitions they seemed to have retreated back into the separatist religious community and many former Levellers and Diggers eventually found a home in the early Quaker movement.

64. The Banning of Christmas Provoked Riots

Previously we discussed godly reformation and the Parliamentary and Puritan attack upon the traditional ritual year and popular sports and pastimes. We have also seen how the period 1646–47 was a time of growing disillusionment in the country over the failure to reach a settlement with the King and continuing high taxation to finance the army. In June 1647, Parliament passed an ordinance formally abolishing Christmas, Easter, Whitsuntide and all holy days traditionally observed. On Christmas Day 1647, riots broke out in Ipswich and Canterbury when the authorities tried to forbid Christmas celebrations. In Canterbury the rioters drove the mayor and several Puritan magistrates and ministers out of the city and the Kent Trained Bands were called in to restore order. In London, in January 1648, there were tax riots and the MPs in Parliament requested troops from Fairfax for their protection. At the end of March, the King's accession day was celebrated enthusiastically in London and in many towns across England, the mayor of Norwich being particularly enthusiastic in ordering bonfires and feasting to mark the event. The following month rioting in London became so serious that the Lord Mayor took refuge in the Tower. A combination of war-weariness, resentment at high taxes and anger over the continual attacks upon 'merrie England' finally brought many people, who had once been sympathetic to Parliament, to contemplate resistance or even outright rebellion. This was a situation the King and the Royalists hoped to exploit to their advantage, but it is worth considering whether resistance to Parliamentary taxes and ordinances automatically meant support for the King; could resistance not have been as much anti-Parliament as pro-King? Meanwhile, Charles had been secretly negotiating with anti-Covenanting Scots and in December 1647 he signed a treaty with them called the Engagement. By this, the Scots would invade England, rescue the King and, along with English Royalists who were expected to rise up in large numbers, restore Charles and defeat the Parliamentarians and the New Model. In return, Charles agreed to allow a three-year trial of Presbyterianism in England (as long as he and his family could remain Anglicans), after which there would be a comprehensive and negotiated settlement of the religious question.

65. The Scots Invaded England In 1648

Events in Scotland had moved rapidly since the end of the first Civil War and, as we have just seen, different factions had emerged in Edinburgh, principally, those who remained loyal to the treaty of 1643 with the English Parliament, led by Archibald Campbell, first Marquess of Argyll, and the majority of the Kirk – known as Covenanters - and those who favoured the recently agreed Engagement with the King, led by James Hamilton, 1st Duke of Hamilton, who were known as the Engagers.

With the Engagers in the ascendant in early 1648, preparations were made to raise an army to invade England and rescue the King. The border towns of Berwick and Carlisle were seized by local Royalists to facilitate a Scottish invasion, and on 8 July Hamilton's army crossed the border and entered Carlisle.

The Parliamentarian commander in the north was Major-General John Lambert. Lambert was not strong enough to face Hamilton's forces alone so he withdrew into County Durham to await the arrival of Cromwell and reinforcements. Lambert and Cromwell rendezvoused at Wetherby in Yorkshire on 13 August. Meanwhile, Hamilton had marched south into Lancashire hoping that local Royalists would join him. Cromwell and Lambert crossed the Pennines in pursuit.

Unaware of the proximity of the New Model, Hamilton's army was strung out in a line between Preston and Wigan, and it was at Preston on 17 August 1648 that Cromwell and Lambert encountered the Engager infantry and their Royalist allies under Sir Marmaduke Langdale. In the ensuing battle the Engagers and Royalists were defeated and Cromwell occupied Preston. The remainder of the Engager army retreated south, pursued by Cromwell and Lambert, through Wigan and towards Warrington where, on the 19th, at the Battle of Winwick Pass, they were also defeated. Langdale was captured near Nottingham and Hamilton surrendered to Lambert at Uttoxeter in Staffordshire on the 25th. Meanwhile Cromwell marched north to Scotland to try and overthrow the Engager government in Edinburgh. A major threat to the English Parliament had been neutralised by the New Model.

66. The New Model Army Called Charles a 'Man of Blood'

When the news broke that Charles had signed the Engagement with a faction of the Scots who planned to invade England, there was anger and a deep sense of outrage in Parliament and the army at what he had done. Not only was it clear that Charles was prepared to countenance further bloodshed, it also demonstrated that he had no intention of negotiating a lasting settlement with his enemies and that his word could not be trusted. With rebellions and riots spreading across England and the prospect of a Scottish invasion, the New Model prepared itself once more for action. In late April 1648, the army met at Windsor for a great prayer meeting, during which they resolved to bring 'Charles Stuart, that man of blood, to an account for that blood he had shed and mischief he had done to his utmost against the Lord's cause and people in these poor nations'. Ever since the war began in 1642 Parliament and the army had officially claimed that they fought for 'the King and Parliament'. They blamed the war not on Charles but on his close advisors, his 'evil counsellors', who were misleading the King and giving him the wrong advice. The fiction of the 'evil counsellors' meant that Parliament did not have to make the King personally responsible for the war.

But the Engagement and the events of 1648 changed all this and, at the prayer meeting, the army for the first time pointed the finger of accusation squarely at Charles, saying that he was personally responsible for the start of the war and for trying to bring the Scots into England to renew the conflict. He was 'a man of blood' and as such he must be brought to trial for causing and prolonging the war. Even the conservative gentlemen of the House of Commons, incensed by the Engagement, voted on

3 January 1648 not to negotiate any further with Charles. Yet if they were not going to negotiate with him, what was Parliament going to do with the King? As the siege of Colchester reached its climax in late August the ever cautious Commons repealed the Vote of No Addresses and prepared to send another group of commissioners to the Isle of Wight to reopen negotiations with the King. News of the repeal of No Addresses was greeted with shock and disbelief in the army and by many in the Parliamentarian camp. The Engagement and the Scottish invasion had convinced many, Cromwell included, that Charles was not to be trusted and that he was now the major obstacle to a lasting settlement. Petitions urging 'justice' on the King were drawn up in many quarters and presented to Parliament and the army.

Despite these objections, Parliamentary commissioners arrived on the Isle of Wight on 15 September to negotiate with the King. The demands they presented, known as the Treaty of Newport, were the same as those of Uxbridge, Newcastle and the Four Bills and even now Charles prevaricated in his replies. The negotiations dragged on through October, but in the army anger at Parliament's conduct mounted until, in early November, Fairfax summoned a General Council of the army to St Albans. At the council Ireton presented the *Army Remonstrance* demanding the purging of Parliament and the trial of the King. This, after much debate, was adopted on the 18th.

Meanwhile the Commons agreed to the King's request to return to London 'in honour, freedom and safety' at the conclusion of the negotiations at Newport. On the 20th the *Army Remonstrance* was presented to Parliament, who decided to defer consideration of it until after the King had signed the Treaty of Newport. On the 24th the army headquarters were moved from St Albans to Windsor and on the 27th the Parliamentary commissioners returned from Newport and presented the King's replies to Parliament's proposals. Parliament again decided to defer consideration of the *Remonstrance* until they had heard and debated the King's replies. Frustrated at being ignored, the army resolved to occupy London to force consideration of the *Remonstrance*. Finally, on the 30th, Parliament debated the *Remonstrance* and voted to reject it by a sizeable majority. On 2 December the army marched into London.

67. Fairfax Defeated the Royalists at Colchester

We saw how the riots and rebellions of 1648 began in Canterbury and Ipswich over the banning of Christmas and how the Mayor of Norwich, in a deliberately provocative gesture, authorised celebrations to mark the King's accession in March. On 28 April rioting broke out in Norwich in support of the Mayor, when he was ordered to appear before the Commons to explain his actions. The rioters captured and imprisoned the Norfolk County Committee as well as seizing the county magazine, which then exploded, destroying or damaging a large area of the city and killing over 100 people. On 4 May over 2,000 petitioners from Essex descended on Westminster, calling on Parliament to restore the King and disband the army. On the 11th a Grand Jury in Canterbury dismissed all charges against those who had taken part in the Christmas riots and a petition similar to that from Essex was prepared. The following day, Royalist rioters in Bury St Edmunds seized the county magazine and had to be dispersed by troops, and on the 16th there were further disturbances in Westminster when petitioners from Surrey tried to present their petition to Parliament. This evidence of widespread discontent in the counties surrounding London and East Anglia was particularly significant as these areas had always been the heartlands of the Parliamentarian cause. East Anglia, in particular, was the home of Cromwell, the Eastern Association and the New Model Army. Now, deep in the Parliamentarian heartlands, voices were raised in complaint and active resistance was being offered to Parliament.

On 21 May rebellion flared up in Kent when the county committee tried to suppress the county's petition. Rochester, Sittingbourne, Faversham and Sandwich were seized in the King's name and the insurgents agreed to rendezvous at Blackheath to present their petition to Parliament. They also contacted naval officers and sailors stationed around the Kent coast and a large number of ships defected to them, allowing them to take control of the coastal fortresses of Sandown, Deal and Walmer. Meanwhile the insurgents had taken Dartford, Deptford and the naval dockyards at Chatham.

The task of facing the Kentish rebels fell to Fairfax, and with his approach the insurgents abandoned Deptford and fell back on Dartford, appointing the Royalist George Goring, the 1st Earl of Norwich, as their leader. Fairfax moved into Kent and marched towards Maidstone where, on 1 June, the insurgent forces were decisively beaten. The Earl of Norwich escaped the battle and headed for London, pursued by cavalry from the New Model. He was saved from capture by the fact that, on 4 June, Essex rose in revolt, led by Sir Charles Lucas of Colchester. The Earl of Norwich, with 500 supporters, crossed the Thames into Essex and linked up with Lucas's forces. Meanwhile the final group of Kentish insurgents surrendered at Canterbury on the 8th.

Back in Essex, Sir George Lisle and other prominent Royalists joined Sir Charles Lucas's forces at Chelmsford. Thwarted in their attempt to seize the county magazine at Braintree, and aware that Fairfax had crossed the Thames and entered the county, they fell back on Colchester. There they hoped to recruit more men and, if the worst happened, escape down the River Colne and across to Holland. In the event, Colchester was to be the place where another major threat to Parliament was to be destroyed.

When Fairfax laid siege to Colchester on 13 June 1648, its defenders had a reasonable hope that their cause could yet prosper. In south Wales, Colonel Poyer held

Pembroke Castle for the King and the Duke of Hamilton was preparing a large Engager army with which to invade England and rescue Charles. Nearer home there were encouraging signs of disaffection with Parliament, such as the 'battle' of Linton in Essex on 16 June, when Royalists and Parliamentarians fought each other through the village. But the fatal flaw in all these actions was that they were not coordinated. This enabled Fairfax, Cromwell and the New Model to pick off each rebellion, revolt or invasion one by one. Soon after Fairfax arrived before Colchester the defenders realised that they were trapped when the mouth of the River Colne was successfully blockaded by Parliamentarian ships while the Suffolk Trained Bands secured the roads leading north out of Colchester. After an unsuccessful initial assault Fairfax settled down for a long siege, throwing up barricades and forts around the town and bringing up his heavy artillery.

The defenders put up a spirited resistance, mounting guns on the tops of the church towers with which to fire over the walls and into the enemy camp. But gradually they were pushed back. On 14 July Fairfax gained the Hythe, the harbour of the town, and the Abbey Gatehouse (a defensive position to the south of the town) also fell. By August the defenders and townsfolk were in a desperate situation: starving, running low on ammunition and with no hope of relief or rescue. When news came through of the defeat of Hamilton and the Engagers at Preston, Lisle and Lucas realised that it was useless to continue the fight. On 27 August, Colchester surrendered to Fairfax and, two days later, Lisle and Lucas were condemned by a court martial and executed by firing squad outside Colchester Castle.

68. MICHAEL HUDSON HAD HIS HANDS CUT OFF

The second Civil War was fought with a ferocity that was rare in the first war. In 1648, defeated forces were often treated very harshly and their commanders sometimes executed. One example of this is the fate of Michael Hudson. He was born in 1605, attended Oxford and became a clergyman. When war broke out in 1642 Hudson joined the Royalists, was present at Edgehill and afterwards moved to Oxford where he became a royal chaplain. He was appointed Scout Master to the Marquess of Newcastle and may have been present at Marston Moor.

When Charles decided to quit Oxford in April 1646, he chose Hudson and John Ashburnham to accompany him; Hudson was also present when the King surrendered to the Scots at Southwell. Parliament demanded that Hudson be handed over to them, but the Scots refused and released him. Unfortunately, while trying to escape to France, Hudson was arrested at Sandwich and imprisoned in London. In June 1646, he was examined by a committee of Parliament and gave them a detailed account of the King's journey from Oxford to Southwell. In November he escaped from Parliament's custody and became a Royalist agent, smuggling letters to and from the King. In January 1647, he was captured again at Hull and imprisoned in the Tower. He remained there for about a year before again escaping in early 1648 disguised as an apple seller.

Returning to Lincolnshire he worked to raise the Royalist gentry there and in East Anglia. With a troop of Royalist horse he eventually took refuge in Woodcroft House, Northamptonshire, a strongly built manor house surrounded by a moat. The house was shortly afterwards besieged by a Parliamentarian force. Hudson defended the house well, but eventually the enemy forced their way in and the remaining Royalists were finally cornered on the roof. At this point it seems that they were promised quarter if they surrender, which they did. However, the promise of quarter was not kept. Hudson was thrown over the battlements but managed to grab onto a waterspout or projecting stone to stop himself falling. At this point the Parliamentarian soldiers cut off his hands and he fell. Using his stumps he swam ashore but was met by another group of soldiers who clubbed him to death with their musket butts. It is said that his tongue was then cut out and carried as a trophy by the victorious Parliamentarians, but this may be a Royalist atrocity story. Whether Hudson lost his tongue or not, the manner of his death at Woodcroft illustrates that the war in 1648 was conducted with a savagery rarely seen between 1642 and 1646.

69. PRINCE RUPERT BECAME A PRIVATEER

With the defeat of the Royalists in 1646, Rupert and Maurice returned to the Netherlands. Two years later, during the second Civil War, part of the English fleet mutinied, as we have seen, and declared for the King, eleven ships sailed to the Netherlands and eventually placed themselves under Rupert's command. Initially, it was unclear how the Royalists should use this new fleet. Some wanted to help the Scots who were fighting Parliament, some wanted to storm the Isle of Wight and rescue Charles I, while others wanted to blockade the mouth of the Thames. The swift defeat of the various risings in England and of the Scots at Preston made all these plans redundant and the fleet returned to the Netherlands. Royalist forces were still active in Ireland under the Marquess of Ormonde and in January 1649 Rupert and Maurice sailed to Kinsale from where they preyed on English shipping in the Irish Sea. But Cromwell's victories in Ireland in late 1649 forced Rupert to abandon Kinsale.

Rupert and Maurice could have returned to the Netherlands, but they had a more daring plan and sailed for Lisbon, which they hoped would provide a base from which they could continue to prey on the ships of the new English Commonwealth. Unfortunately, the English forced the Portuguese government to expel Rupert and his fleet. He headed for the Mediterranean where he continued to harry English shipping. From there he sailed down the coast of west Africa, attacking shipping and bases until, in the summer of 1652, it was decided to sail across the Atlantic and link up with Royalists in Barbados. By now Rupert and Maurice only had four ships that were seaworthy and before they could arrive Barbados had fallen to Commonwealth forces. To make matters worse, Rupert lost two further ships in violent storms along with his beloved younger brother, Maurice. Grief-stricken and demoralised Rupert sailed back to Europe, eventually arriving in a French port, ill and exhausted, in March 1653. Between 1649 and 1653, Rupert, Maurice and their small fleet had sailed over 15,000 miles and taken over thirty prizes.

70. The New Model Army Staged a Military Coup

Earlier we saw how the army were dismayed by Parliament's decision to resume negotiations with the King after the victories they had achieved in the second Civil War. We have also seen how the resolution of the Windsor prayer meeting in April and the Remonstrance of November held Charles personally responsible for the war and demanded that he be brought to justice, demands that were largely ignored by Parliament. Frustrated by the lack of response to their demands and fearful that Parliament would proceed to a compromise peace with the King early December saw the confrontation between the army and Parliament come to a head.

On 1 December when the army moved Charles from Carisbrooke Castle on the Isle of Wight to Hurst Castle, a bleak fortress on the Hampshire coast, he was convinced that he had been taken there to be murdered. Parliament reprimanded Fairfax for moving the King without their authorisation and on 5 December proceeded to declare that the King's latest response to the negotiations at Newport were sufficient to proceed to a final treaty. This vote provoked the army into action and on the morning of 6 December the MPs arriving at the Parliament house found the doors blocked by a detachment of soldiers led by Colonel Thomas Pride. Pride was accompanied by a few Independent MPs and had lists of names in his hand. As the MPs attempted to enter, their names were checked against the lists. Those deemed sympathetic to the army were allowed to enter Parliament. Those deemed hostile to the army were denied entry. Of around 470 MPs Pride's Purge removed around 270 and another 100 MPs refused to attend the House in protest. Only around 100 MPs were left to put the army's resolutions into effect and this truncated Parliament was very soon christened 'the Rump'.

The purged Parliament soon proceeded to reject the treaty of Newport and began to prepare the way for the trial of the King. By 22 December Charles had been moved from Hurst Castle to Windsor and on 6 January 1649 Parliament passed an ordinance establishing a High Court of Justice to try the King. Before that, on the 4th, they had declared themselves to be the sole, legitimate authority within the kingdom in the following words:

> The Commons of England assembled in Parliament declare that the people under God are the origin of all just power: and do also declare, that the Commons of England assembled in Parliament, being chosen by and representing the people, have the supreme authority in this nation: and do also declare, that whatsoever is enacted and declared law by the Commons of England assembled in Parliament, hath the force of law, and all the people of this nation are included thereby, although the consent and concurrence of the King and the House of Peers be not had thereunto.*

*Declaration of the House of Commons, 4 January 1649, in *House of Commons Journal*, Vol. 6, pp. 110–111.

71. The King Was Tried In Westminster Hall

On 19 January 1649, Charles was brought from Windsor to St James's Palace and the following day lodged at the house of Sir Robert Cotton at Westminster where he could be more easily guarded. Shortly after 2 p.m. on Saturday the 20th the President of the High Court of Justice, John Bradshaw, took his seat in Westminster Hall and the court commenced its work. When the King was brought in the charge against him was read out by the prosecutor, John Cook. The charge reiterated what the army had said at the Windsor prayer meeting, that Charles, 'hath been, and is, the occasioner, author and continuer of the said unnatural, cruel and bloody wars; and therein guilty of all the treasons, murders, rapines, burnings, spoils, desolations, damages and mischiefs to this nation, acted and committed in the said wars, or occasioned thereby'. The reason why Charles had unleashed the war was to make himself a tyrant and overturn the constitution of the kingdom. In so doing, he had broken the contract between himself and his people, which required him to rule for the good of the people and uphold their traditional laws and liberties. The charge also called the King, 'Charles Stuart, being admitted King of England', a grudging acknowledgement that while he might be king he was just a man called Charles Stuart, like any other man summoned to account before a court of law. The charge thus stripped Charles of the aura of divine right power and asserted that his rule was grounded in the contract between himself and the nation, to whom he was accountable, rather than bestowed upon him by the grace of God.*

But however much the charge might reject the notion of sacred monarchy and hold Charles responsible for the war, from the beginning things did not go well for Bradshaw and the court. Instead of entering a plea Charles asked by what lawful authority he was tried, if the court could answer that question to his satisfaction he would then enter a plea. Bradshaw seemed surprised by this question and replied that the court sat in the name of 'the people of England'. A reply that did not impress the King, and Bradshaw adjourned the court until Monday. When the court reassembled the confrontation between Charles and Bradshaw continued, with Charles insisting that the court had no legitimate authority to try him, while Bradshaw contended that it had. The second day of the trial ended in a stalemate, as did the third. On Wednesday 24th the court heard witnesses against the King in private and the following day resolved that there was enough evidence to sentence the King to death; the wording of the sentence was agreed on the 25th.

The court reassembled on Saturday 26th, but when Bradshaw tried to open the proceedings he was heckled by a masked lady in one of the public galleries – was this masked woman Lady Fairfax? Proceedings were further interrupted by one of the judges, John Downes, who declared himself dissatisfied with the proceedings. The court adjourned to hear Downes's objections, which were quickly brushed aside. On reassembling, Bradshaw proceeded to his summing-up of the case and, finally, condemned Charles to death as a traitor and tyrant. Charles tried to speak, but was silenced and then led away to St James's.

*Gardiner, S. R., *The Constitutional Documents of the Puritan Revolution 1625–1660*, 3rd edition (Oxford: Clarendon Press, 1906), pp. 371–74.

72. The Refusal to Remove One's Hat Could Be a Political Gesture

In the mid-seventeenth century everyone wore a hat and there was a complex etiquette of removing, or doffing, one's hat to one's social superiors, to ladies, before courts of law, etc. 'Hat honour', as it was called, was important in maintaining accepted codes of deference in a status society. But it could also be used to make political gestures, two examples will suffice to illustrate this, both from 1649. The first occurred when Charles was seated facing his judges in Westminster Hall, it was noted by commentators that he did not remove his hat when taking his place. This was a deliberate gesture on Charles's part, it demonstrated his contempt for the court and its proceedings as an illegitimate charade created by a usurping power. The other incident occurred the following April when the Digger leaders, Gerrard Winstanley and William Everard, were granted an interview in Whitehall with the Lord General, Thomas Fairfax. Winstanley and Everard wanted to explain to Fairfax why they and their followers had commenced digging up the common land at St George's Hill, and perhaps gain his patronage and protection. As their social superior and commander of the New Model Army it would have been expected for them to remove their hats in Fairfax's presence, but it was observed that they failed to do so throughout the interview. When questioned as to why they had not removed their hats they replied that the Lord General was, 'but their fellow creature'. In other words, neither Winstanley nor Everard acknowledged the social hierarchy and the etiquette that accompanied it. They believed that all men were equal in the sight of God and there was no place for deference and hat honour in an egalitarian and communal society. This commitment to social levelling was soon to be adopted by the Quakers, who also refused all titles, the taking of oaths and hat honour, and who often offended authority in the process.

73. Charles I Was Executed on 30 January 1649

On Sunday 28 January Charles was taken from Whitehall back to St James's Palace where he remained until his execution. He spent his remaining time in prayer and in disposing of his remaining possessions. On Monday Charles bid an emotional farewell to the two of his six children who remained in England: thirteen-year-old Princess Elizabeth and eight-year-old Henry, Duke of Gloucester. By that evening there were fifty-nine signatures on the King's death warrant and his execution was fixed for the following day, Tuesday 30 January.

The 30th was a bitterly cold day and, having dressed and taken communion, Charles awaited his summons. This came just before 10 a.m. and the party left St James's, walking across the park to Whitehall Palace. Charles was now kept waiting for nearly four hours while the Rump rushed through an ordinance making it illegal to proclaim Charles II after his father's execution, before finally being led through the Banqueting House – outside of which the scaffold had been erected. Once on the scaffold, Charles spoke briefly, asserting his innocence of the charges laid against him. It was also clear that he still felt guilty for his betrayal of Strafford back in 1641 for he stated that, 'An unjust sentence that I suffered to take effect, is punished now by an unjust sentence on me.' Charles concluded by stating, 'I have a good cause and a gracious God ... I go from a corruptible to an incorruptible crown, where no disturbance can be, no disturbance in the world.'* With that he knelt down and placing his head on the block, the headsman struck it off with one blow.

*Wedgwood, C. V., *The Trial of Charles I* (London: Collins, 1964), pp. 190, 192.

74. SOME HONOURED CHARLES AS 'KING AND MARTYR'

Charles was buried on 9 February at St George's Chapel, Windsor. On the same day a small book appeared for sale in London called *Eikon Basilike: The Portraiture of his Sacred Majesty in his Solitudes and Sufferings*. The book purported to be written by the King himself during his captivity, and in twenty-eight chapters gave his version of events since the calling of the Long Parliament in 1640. Most of the twenty-eight chapters concluded with prayers and meditations, which transformed the book into a devotional work. The book was an immediate success, and in the course of the next twelve months went through more than thirty-nine editions and printings. After the Bible and the *Book of Common Prayer*, the *Eikon Basilike* was the bestselling book of the seventeenth century. The authorities tried to suppress the book and commissioned John Milton to write an attack upon it, which he did in a book called *Eikonoklastes* ('the image breaker'). But the authorities could not challenge the image of Charles presented in the *Eikon Basilike* as a gentle, moderate man, suffering on behalf of his people. The frontispiece, in particular, sums up the image of Charles contained in the book, showing the King as a Christian martyr, patiently enduring his Passion and following in the footsteps of Christ.

75. The Rump Parliament and the Army Soon Consolidated Their Power

With the King dead, the Rump Parliament and the army moved quickly to consolidate the new order. From now on legislative power lay solely with the House of Commons, which, on 13 February created an executive body called the Council of State, with John Bradshaw as president and, de facto, head of state. On 17 March the monarchy was formally abolished, as was the House of Lords two days later. But it was not until 19 May that Parliament officially proclaimed England a 'Commonwealth and Free State'.

The new Commonwealth was defended in print by John Milton, who in February published *The Tenure of Kings and Magistrates*, a spirited defence of the right of resistance to tyranny and the freedom of men to choose their rulers. However, an alternative view of recent events was given by John Lilburne who, in the same month, published *England's New Chains Discovered* in which he criticised the Rump for betraying the 'good old cause' by failing to institute a wide-ranging programme of reform. Lilburne claimed that the execution of the King had achieved nothing and now the Rump and the army were busy forging 'new chains' with which to bind the people.

76. The Execution of the King Was the End of Revolution

The events of December 1648–January 1649 were truly revolutionary. An army coup, the purging of Parliament and the trial and execution of the King turned the world upside down in a way no one could have imagined possible back in 1642. Many contemporaries, including, as we have just seen, John Lilburne, hoped that these events marked the beginning of the longed-for 'time of shaking', which would usher in the New Jerusalem and the advent of their millenarian and reforming hopes and ambitions.

Yet some historians have argued that the events between Pride's Purge and the regicide were the culmination of revolution rather than the dawn of a new millennium and that the army Grandees who sent Charles to his death intended this as a way of containing rather than encouraging further radical change. It has been said that the problem with the 'English Revolution' was that its leaders were not revolutionaries! This is a question we will look at as we consider the Commonwealth, the Protectorate and how Oliver Cromwell became Lord Protector of England.

77. Cromwell Is Not Popular In the Republic of Ireland

The new Commonwealth faced three main challenges: within England there were the Levellers, while externally there were the Scots and the Irish. Disappointment at the lack of reform caused Leveller-inspired mutinies to break out in certain regiments of the New Model Army. Cromwell moved quickly to crush these mutinies and re-establish discipline. Events in Ireland were not so easily solved.

Ever since the Irish Rebellion of October 1641 the majority of Ireland had been in the hands of a native, Catholic government called the Confederation. During the Civil War, Charles had tried to ally with the Confederates to bring over an Irish army to fight for him in England. With the establishment of the Commonwealth the Rump was eager to crush the Confederation and bring Ireland back under English rule, and in August 1649 Cromwell was dispatched to Ireland to do just that. The forces of the Confederation and their Royalist allies were no match for the New Model. At the beginning of September, Cromwell besieged Drogheda; when the defenders refused to surrender, the town was taken by storm and many of the inhabitants were put to the sword. The same thing happened a month later at Wexford. Although the massacres at Drogheda and Wexford have tarnished Cromwell's reputation, and although the campaign in Ireland was fought with a ferocity unknown in England, in the short term it was very effective. By the time Cromwell left Ireland in May 1650, most of Ulster, Leinster and Munster were firmly in English hands. Cromwell's son-in-law, Ireton, was left as Lord Deputy of Ireland with instructions to continue the war until the Confederates and their Royalist allies were defeated, a process that took until May 1652 to complete.

78. CROMWELL INVADED SCOTLAND TO PERSUADE THEM TO ABANDON THE STUARTS

In 1648, the Covenanters in Scotland had aided the English Parliament in its struggle with the Engagers but, after the execution of Charles I and the establishment of the Commonwealth, relations rapidly cooled between London and Edinburgh. The Scots were outraged that the English had executed Charles – who was also King of Scots – without consulting them. They were also profoundly unhappy that the new regime in England was based on Independent principles of religious anathema to the Presbyterian Kirk.

In May 1650 the exiled Charles II, Charles I's eldest son and heir, concluded an alliance with the Scottish Covenanters and the following month landed in Scotland and declared himself a Presbyterian by taking the covenant. By his treaty with the Covenanters Charles also repudiated the Royalists in Ireland and abandoned the Earl of Montrose, who was leading Royalist resistance in the Highlands; such actions dismayed and alienated many loyal Royalists. With the threat of a Scottish Royalist invasion a distinct possibility, the Rump decided on a pre-emptive strike, and as Sir Thomas Fairfax was reluctant to command the army against the Presbyterian Scots, he resigned in favour of Cromwell, who was appointed Captain-General of the New Model on 26 June.

Cromwell crossed the border the following month and it is noticeable how different his tactics were against the – to him – misguided but Protestant Scots as opposed to the Catholic Irish. In Ireland, Cromwell descended with fire and sword, but in Scotland he tried to negotiate and sought to detach the Covenanters from their alliance with Charles II. The Covenanters were not convinced and sought to defeat the English army at Dunbar on 3 September. Their attempt failed, and Dunbar is often cited as one of Cromwell's most brilliant victories. By the end of 1650 Cromwell had occupied Edinburgh.

Meanwhile, the Covenanters and Charles II were still active in the central Highlands and 1651 dawned with Charles being crowned 'King of Scots' at Scone. Negotiations dragged on inconclusively through the first half of 1651 until in August Cromwell feigned a march on Perth, which left the west of Scotland and the border with England open. Charles and his Scottish allies saw their chance and took it, marching south into England. Cromwell at once abandoned the march on Perth and set off in pursuit. Charles hoped that his presence would inspire a Royalist uprising in England.

79. Charles II Disliked His Time in Scotland

Charles II's actions in turning his back on his most loyal and able followers and taking the Presbyterian Covenant was only the beginning of a miserable time in Scotland between April 1650 and August 1651. Charles had already demonstrated in exile that he was a very different character to his chaste and pious father. He enjoyed a good party and had already taken a mistress called Lucy Walter at The Hague who gave birth to his eldest illegitimate child, the future James, Duke of Monmouth, in April 1649. On arrival in Scotland Charles soon found himself surrounded by some of the most hard line of the Presbyterians, whose dour ministers took a very dim view of Charles's propensities. Although he was nominally king, Charles was left in no doubt where the real power resided. Instead of parties and pretty women Charles was forced to listen to interminable sermons from preachers who had an insatiable appetite for the sound of their own voices. On one occasion Charles complained bitterly that he was obliged to listen to six sermons in one day. The preachers waxed lyrical on his personal sins and failings, calling on him over and over again to abase himself before God and the Kirk, confess his sins and beg for forgiveness. They delighted in castigating his mother who, as a Roman Catholic, was of the Devil's brood and his father for the heinous sin of refusing to sign the Covenant. They also purged Charles's court of his followers: Cavaliers, Anglicans and anyone whose morals and behaviour fell below the rigorous standards imposed by the Kirk were dismissed. The purge of the court and the army was so thorough that it has been said that the army which faced Cromwell at Dunbar was half army and half Presbyterian prayer meeting. Charles soon came to loathe what he described as the villainy and hypocrisy of the Covenanters, remarking later that Presbyterianism was no religion for a gentleman! He looked forward to marching into England where he hoped not only to win back his crown but also free himself from the oppression of his Scottish minders.

80. The Scots Invaded England in 1651

Charles II and his Covenanting allies marched south into England in August 1651 with a force around 14,000 strong. The plan was that when English Royalists and Presbyterians heard that the King was in England with a large army they would rush forward to join him and, with overwhelming force, Charles would descend on London and sweep away the Commonwealth; unfortunately for Charles, in the event very few turned out to join him. To most of the English a Scottish army in England meant invasion rather than liberation, also many were sick of the war and not prepared to risk either themselves, their families or their property in what might be a lost cause. Instead of striking at London, Charles remained in the west, marching south along the Welsh border until he reached Worcester on 22 August. A few days later came the news that a small Royalist force raised in Lancashire had been defeated at Wigan.

Meanwhile, the New Model Army was on the march. Cromwell marched back into England, Major-General Lambert shadowed the Scots and Royalists as they marched south and was joined by Major-General Harrison at Preston. Major-General Fleetwood led a detachment from London that rendezvoused with Cromwell, Lambert and Harrison at Warwick; at the same time, Major-General Desborough marched from the south-west towards Worcester. By the time the combined forces of the New Model arrived before Worcester it was a mighty force of around 28,000 regular soldiers and cavalry with a further 3,000 militiamen, facing it was a Scottish-Royalist force of around 16,000.

The Battle of Worcester on 3 September was bitter and bloody. Despite overwhelming numbers Cromwell had to contend with a well-entrenched enemy and also had to somehow cross the rivers Severn and Teme using pontoon bridges. The Scots and Royalists fought bravely but the force of numbers could not stop the enemy crossing the rivers and, eventually, they were driven back into the city where the fighting became hand-to-hand in the narrow streets. Charles and his commanders attempted to rally their men but panic began to take hold and when it was clear that all was lost Charles was persuaded to escape. Around 3,000 Scots and Royalists were killed at Worcester and another 10,000 were taken prisoner, of whom many were sold into indentured labour and shipped to the American colonies and Barbados.

Charles and a few companions tried to escape to the Continent. The Commonwealth put a price of £1000 on his head and in the wanted poster he was described as 'a black man two yards tall' – Charles was tall for the period and had jet-black hair and swarthy looks. Aided by loyalist gentry, many of them Roman Catholics, Charles was passed from safe house to safe house in an attempt to get him out of the country. In the process he disguised himself as a servant and, on one famous occasion, hid in an oak tree in Boscobel wood in Shropshire. It took him six weeks to reach the south coast from where he eventually found a boat to take him into exile; he was to remain in exile for another nine years. Worcester finally destroyed the Royalist cause in England and Cromwell, reflecting on the great victory, called it 'the crowning mercy'.

81. THE COMMONWEALTH PASSED THE FIRST ACT OR ORDINANCE OF PARLIAMENT IN ENGLISH HISTORY GUARANTEEING RELIGIOUS TOLERATION

We have seen how the army first proposed religious toleration in the 'Heads of the Proposals' back in 1647 and the ways in which this grew out of the logic of the Independent vision of liberty of conscience and the first act establishing religious toleration was passed in September 1650. In the act, Parliament repealed and abolished, 'all and every the branches, clauses, articles and provisos expressed and contained in any other act or ordinance of Parliament, whereby or wherein any penalty or punishment is imposed, or mentioned to be imposed on any person whatsoever, for not repairing to their respective parish churches, or for not keeping of holy days, or for not hearing Common Prayer, or for speaking or inveighing against the *Book of Common Prayer*, shall be, and are by the authority aforesaid, wholly repealed and made void'.

But while Parliament wished to free the godly from religious persecution for dissenting from the Church of England and its liturgy, they were determined that this liberty should not be abused by 'profane or licentious persons' who might use the newly granted liberty to neglect their religious duties entirely. Therefore, the act enjoined that on Sundays all should engage in some form of Protestant worship in a public place, either in their parish church, or, should they so choose, 'at some other place in the practice of some religious duty, either of prayer, preaching, reading or expounding the scriptures, or conferring upon the same'.* Liberty was granted to the orthodox Protestant conscience to worship God in any way it deemed appropriate, what was not granted was the liberty to withdraw from honouring God in some form or another.

Gardiner, S. R., *The Constitutional Documents of the Puritan Revolution 1625–1660*, 3rd edition (Oxford: Clarendon Press, 1906), pp. 393, 394.

82. The Nominated Assembly Was Known as 'Barebone's Parliament'

With the defeat of the Commonwealth's enemies, both internal and external, many hoped that the Rump would address itself to solving some of the urgent social and political problems remaining from the Civil War. But although the MPs in the Commons did a great deal of talking and set up a great many committees, very little actual reform was forthcoming. Calls were heard on many sides for such things as reform of the voting system and reform of the law, and many, particularly in the army, were concerned that the Rump was becoming a self-perpetuating civilian oligarchy. In May 1652, trade rivalries with the Dutch erupted in the First Dutch War, fought mainly at sea. As 1653 dawned, frustration at the Rump's inertia increased until, on 20 April, Cromwell arrived at the House of Commons with a detachment of soldiers and forcibly ejected the MPs, telling them that they had 'sat too long for any good you have been doing lately'. Writing to her fiancé, William Temple, on 23 April Dorothy Osborne remarked, 'Bless me, what will become of us all now? Is not this a strange turn? ... Well, 'tis a pleasant world this. If Mr Pym were alive again I wonder what he would think of these proceedings, and whether this would appear as great a breach of the privileges of Parliament as the demanding [of] the five members.'* Cromwell was to prove as efficient as Charles I in turning out Parliaments!

Cromwell was now the most powerful man in the country. With the army at his back he could have made himself dictator or even king; he did neither of these things. Instead, in consultation with the Council of Officers, leading Independent ministers and some former Independent MPs, he arranged for invitations to be sent out to the Independent congregations and the army to nominate delegates to attend a new assembly. This nominated assembly met on 4 July and has come to be called 'Barebone's Parliament' after one of its members who gloried in the name of Praise-God Barebone! Cromwell had high hopes for this new assembly, seeing it as the force that would finally settle the country on foundations of godliness and true religion. But the initial enthusiasm soon evaporated. Barebone's faced all the same problems that had confronted the Rump, quite apart from the fact that most people in the country considered that it had even less legitimacy than the Rump itself. After six months of fruitless and frustrating existence the members of the assembly resigned their power back into the hands of Cromwell and the army on 12 December.

*Morrill, J. (ed.), *Oliver Cromwell and the English Revolution* (London: Longman, 1990), pp. 91–92.

83. ENGLAND'S FIRST WRITTEN CONSTITUTIONS GUARANTEED RELIGIOUS LIBERTY

Within a week of the resignation of Barebone's Parliament the Council of Officers brought forward a new constitution that appointed Cromwell as Lord Protector. Following on from the act of September 1650, both 'The Instrument of Government' of December 1653 and the 'Humble Petition and Advice' of May 1657 included clauses guaranteeing liberty of conscience. The Instrument of Government declared that all, 'such as profess faith in God by Jesus Christ (though differing in judgment from the doctrine, worship or discipline publically held forth)' were to be protected in this freedom as long as they did not disturb the public peace.

As a result of the James Naylor case – to be discussed next – the Humble Petition and Advice sought to define more closely the boundaries of the permitted toleration. To begin with, Article 11, which deals with this question, is six times longer than that in the Instrument. It begins with a long statement of what 'the true Protestant Christian religion' is and calls for a Confession of Faith to be drawn up setting out orthodox doctrine, 'according to the rule and warrant of the Scriptures'. It then goes on to declare that once such a confession had been agreed and published it would be an offence to criticise or revile the confession publically and it was to be used as the basis upon which dissenters would be persuaded of the error of their ways, although such persuasion could only be done by 'the example of good conversation'.* While the basic right of toleration for orthodox, peaceable, Protestants was reasserted, it was hedged about with a growing number of conditions and exceptions, which reflects a growing fear of religious anarchy and heterodox beliefs and practices.

Gardiner, S. R., *The Constitutional Documents of the Puritan Revolution 1625–1660*, 3rd edition (Oxford: Clarendon Press, 1906), pp. 416, 454.

84. James Naylor Was Punished For Riding into Bristol on a Donkey

James Naylor (1618–1660) from west Yorkshire, joined the Parliamentarian army in 1643 and was present at the Battle of Dunbar in September 1650. During his time as a soldier he discovered a talent for preaching and on leaving the army in 1651 he returned home and joined an Independent congregation. Shortly afterwards he met the Quaker leader George Fox and was converted. He became convinced that God was calling him to become an itinerant preacher, first in the north of England, then, after 1655, in London. However, disputes arose among the London Quakers and Naylor seems to have attracted a group of women followers who clearly saw him as some sort of prophet. Naylor was persuaded to move to Bristol, where he was soon joined by his female followers. It was in October 1656 that the incident took place that was to make Naylor famous – or infamous, depending on your point of view. On 24 October, in driving rain, Naylor entered Bristol riding a horse, while his companions spread their clothes on the ground before him and sang, 'Holy, holy, holy, Lord God of Sabaoth.' It was clear to all that Naylor was re-enacting Christ's entry into Jerusalem. (Mark 11: 7–11, Luke 19: 35–40, John 12: 12–15) The authorities reacted promptly, arresting Naylor and his companions and charging them with blasphemy.

Naylor was initially tried in Bristol, but many who feared the spread of the Quakers as socially subversive and heretical and who sought to restrict the toleration allowed under the Instrument of Government seized upon the Naylor case and he was summoned to appear before Parliament. There he was convicted of blasphemy and of being 'a grand impostor and seducer of the people'. Having convicted him, Parliament then had to decide on a suitable punishment. The Blasphemy Act of 1650 only prescribed imprisonment for a first offence, but the MPs wanted something more satisfying and fell into a sort of feeding-frenzy as they dreamt up ever more draconian punishments. A motion to sentence Naylor to death was defeated by ninety-six votes to eighty-two, but Parliament wished to make an example of Naylor and send a clear message that the boundaries of the toleration were narrowing. In the end, Naylor was sentenced to be flogged through the streets of London while tied to the end of a cart, he was then to be put in the pillory where his tongue would be bored through with a red-hot iron and his forehead branded with a letter 'B' for 'Blasphemer'. As if this was not enough, he was then to be imprisoned in Bridewell for an indefinite period. Naylor was finally released in September 1659 under a general amnesty for Quaker prisoners, but the effects of his punishment and three years in prison had taken their toll. He died the following year.

85. Religious Toleration Was Not Universal

In all the injunctions to toleration, from the 1650 Act of Parliament to the Humble Petition and Advice, there were a series of exceptions to this right; chief among those excepted were Roman Catholics. Parliament, after legislating the abolition of uniformity and the Prayer Book, demand that provision be made, 'for discovering of Papists and Popish recusants, and for disabling of them, and of all Jesuits or priests from disturbing the State'.* Likewise, the Instrument of Government and the Humble Petition and Advice both explicitly excluded Roman Catholics from the toleration.

Another group excluded were, according to the Instrument and the Humble Petition, those who practised prelacy. This was aimed at those Royalists, such as Sir Robert Shirley, John Evelyn and the ejected Anglican clergy, who, as we will see, maintained the Arminian high church tradition of Charles I and Archbishop Laud and celebrated the banned liturgy of the *Book of Common Prayer.* The authorities made a clear connection between devotion to the Church of England and the Prayer Book and Royalist opposition to the Commonwealth.

A third group was far more nebulous than either the Roman Catholics or the Anglican Royalists, but, to the godly authorities, they posed a very real threat. As we have seen, in the 1650 act they are described as 'profane and licentious persons', and both the Instrument and the Humble Petition excludes those who, 'under the profession of Christ, hold forth and practice licentiousness,' and, probably with James Naylor in mind, the Humble Petition also included those, 'who publish horrid blasphemies'.

Who were these evil livers, and why was it felt that they posed such a threat? We have seen that the breakdown of control by an established, national church had led to a profusion of radical religious groups and heterodox religious beliefs. These included those we have called Antinomians – such as the Ranters and the Quakers, who believed that because they had awoken to the inner light of God within them they were now led by that inner light, which meant they were above considerations of man-made laws and morality. To the orthodox Puritan who observed a strict moral code such beliefs were not only deeply shocking but highly subversive. Shocked pamphleteers took great delight in recounting the supposed antics of these 'licentious' people: their sexual promiscuity, their contempt for authority, their deliberate flouting of every accepted code of moral behaviour. While the Quakers certainly believed they were guided by the inner light and were seen by many as a disruptive force there is little evidence that they indulged in sexual promiscuity, that was an accusation levelled at the Ranters. Whether the Ranters ever existed has been questioned by historians, but they were certainly believed to exist by fearful, conservative men in authority and they took great pains to condemn them.

Gardiner, S. R., *The Constitutional Documents of the Puritan Revolution 1625–1660*, 3rd edition (Oxford: Clarendon Press, 1906), p. 321.

86. Sir Robert Shirley Was Arrested By Cromwell For Building a Church

In 1646, Sir Robert Shirley (1629–56) inherited a baronetcy and estates in Warwickshire as well as the family's principal seat at Staunton Harold, Leicestershire. Too young to fight in the first Civil War, Shirley was an enthusiastic Royalist and, in 1648, during the second Civil War, he confronted the Parliamentarian garrison in nearby Ashby-de-la-Zouch. In 1650, he was arrested and sent to the Tower for his involvement with Staffordshire Royalists and his estates were sequestered. On this occasion, Shirley was soon released and returned to Leicestershire where he again threw himself into the Royalist underground movement, sheltering many deprived Royalist clergy who had been expelled from their livings and who were to rise to prominence in the Restoration Church. Shirley also began stockpiling arms and ammunition at Staunton Harold in preparation for a future Royalist rising against the Commonwealth.

It was during this period that Shirley began to build a church next to his manor house. This was an open and public act of defiance. As we have seen, the structures and hierarchy of the Church of England had been largely dismantled, the Anglican liturgy in the *Book of Common Prayer* banned, and there were even proposals to sell off the now redundant cathedrals for building materials. Shirley's church was intended as an explicit statement of high Anglican resistance. Built in the Gothic style, it has a nave and chancel, with an altar against the east wall and it was intended that the illegal Anglican services would be observed daily.

Shirley was already known to the authorities as a militant Royalist and when the recently appointed Lord Protector Cromwell heard in 1654 that Shirley was building a church he remarked that if Shirley could afford to build a church he could afford to fit out a ship for the navy. Shirley refused and was again arrested and committed to the Tower. His confinement does not appear to have been particularly close as the Royalist underground appointed him a financial agent to raise money for the cause. He also drew up a detailed blueprint for a reformed Royalist organisation based upon the parish and diocesan structures of the beleaguered Church of England. However, on 28 November 1656, Shirley succumbed to disease in the Tower and died, aged just twenty-seven.

In his will he left money to help the Royalist cause and to assist persecuted Anglican clergy; he also left money and detailed instructions for the completion of his church. Buried in the family vault in the nearby church of Breedon-on-the-Hill, his body was transferred in 1661 to his now completed church; he was buried beneath the chancel. Staunton Harold Church, now in the care of the National Trust, is well worth a visit. Not only is it one of the very few churches built in England between 1560 and 1660 it is also an essay in Arminian high Anglicanism written in stone; Charles I and Archbishop Laud would have approved!

When the church was completed, shortly after the Restoration, the following inscription was placed over the west door:

In the year 1653
when all thinges Sacred were throughout ye nation
Either demolished or profaned
Sir Robert Shirley, Barronet,
Founded this church;
Whose singular praise it is,
To have done the best things in ye worst times,
And
Hoped them in the most calamitous.
The righteous shall be had in everlasting remembrance.

87. John Evelyn Was Arrested For Going to Church on Christmas Day

We have seen that Parliament abolished Christmas in 1647 and the attempt to suppress its celebration provoked riots in Canterbury the following December, among other places. We have also seen that, despite intermittent persecution, the Church of England continued to exist underground. On Christmas Day 1657, John Evelyn (1620–1706), a committed Royalist and Anglican, wished to take Holy Communion according to the banned Anglican rite and accompanied by his wife, Mary, they travelled to London to attend Holy Communion in the chapel of Exeter House in the Strand. The celebrant was Peter Gunning (1614–84) who, after the Restoration, was to become, successively, Master of St John's College, Cambridge, and Bishop of Chichester and Ely. In the middle of the service the chapel was surrounded by soldiers and Gunning and the congregation arrested. Evelyn states that they were allowed to finish their service of Holy Communion, although 'these wretched miscreants held their muskets against us as we came up to receive the sacred elements, as if they would have shot us at the altar'.

At the close of the service, Evelyn and others were confined in Exeter House and in the afternoon Colonels Whalley and Goffe, both regicides, both former Major-Generals, both supporters of the Protectorate and related by marriage, arrived to interrogate the prisoners. When Evelyn was called before them they first took his name and address, then asked him why he observed Christmas and used the *Book of Common Prayer* when both were forbidden. They also remarked that the Communion liturgy in the *Book of Common Prayer* was 'but the Mass in English'. They also tried to catch Evelyn out by accusing him of praying for the exiled Charles II. Evelyn replied that they merely prayed for all Christian kings, princes and governors and not specifically for Charles. In the end, Evelyn was released and made it home late on the 26th – 'blessed be God' he wrote with relief. Reflecting on this frightening brush with the power of the Protectoral State, Evelyn observed that his interrogators Whalley and Goffe 'were men of high flight and above Ordinances'.*

*Evelyn, J., *The Diary of John Evelyn*, selected and edited with an introduction by John Bowle (Oxford: Oxford University Press, 1985), 173–4.

88. CROMWELL RESPONDED TO CONSPIRACY AND ATTEMPTED REBELLION BY PLACING THE COUNTRY UNDER MILITARY RULE

Ever since the fall of Colchester in August 1648 Royalists and their allies had been seeking ways to continue the struggle against the victorious Parliament. There had been high hopes that Ireland or Scotland would provide a springboard for operations in England, but these hopes were finally dashed at the Battle of Worcester in September 1651. From then on the Royalists could only plot in exile or maintain a precarious underground existence in England as they worked to bring down the Commonwealth. The other option, which many Royalists adopted, was to sit quietly at home and pray for better times. In exile some Royalist conspirators formed the Sealed Knot to try and coordinate resistance with the underground in England, but its activities were not a great success. From July 1653 the Commonwealth's counter-espionage system was run by John Thurloe (1616–68), who was highly efficient at his job. As Cromwell's spymaster-general he usually knew the conspirators' plans in more detail than they did and was able to pre-empt many attempted acts of assassination and resistance.

With the installation of Cromwell as Lord Protector in December 1653 the names of new opponents and potential conspirators were added to Thurloe's list of enemies. These were the republicans and Commonwealth men, as they were known, who could not accept Cromwell's expulsion of the Rump in April 1653 and who condemned the Protectorate as a betrayal of the 'good old cause' and a retreat back to monarchy. Then there was an assortment of Fifth Monarchists and Levellers who condemned Cromwell for, in their opinion, betraying their hopes of reform or frustrating millenarian ambitions. This disparate opposition group on what we might term the 'left' of the Protectorate – republicans, Commonwealth men, Levellers and Fifth Monarchists – never worked together to coordinate their opposition and were no match for Thurloe and his agents.

In March 1655, a small group of Royalists in Wiltshire staged a rising under Colonel John Penruddock. This was supposed to be just one of a number of risings around the country but, apart from Penruddock's group, the planned risings did not take place and Penruddock's rising was easily crushed. The response of the government was to impose military rule upon England and Wales in the form of the major-generals. The country was divided into twelve districts and each district was run by a major-general – a senior army officer who was, in effect, a military governor. Their job was to root out conspiracy and suppress anti-government activity, raise taxes and implement godly reformation. The government also introduced a decimation tax by which a tenth of all property belonging to convicted Royalists and conspirators was forfeit to the government. The major-generals and the decimation tax were abandoned in January 1657, but the Protectorate had proved its point: with the New Model Army to protect it and with Thurloe's intelligence service, it was well-nigh impossible for its opponents to offer any meaningful resistance.

89. Cromwell Turned Down the Offer of the Crown

As part of the proposals which were eventually adopted as the Humble Petition and Advice, Cromwell was offered the crown of England, Scotland and Ireland. He would become Oliver I and the succession would be vested in the Cromwell family. Cromwell refused the offer, but only after two months of discussion and prayer on the subject, which suggests that he did more than consider the proposal. His decision to refuse came after lengthy consultations with senior army officers and ministers of the independent churches, the main constituencies who made up the Protectoral establishment. What the majority of these people told Cromwell was that to accept the crown was to betray the 'good old cause', which they had fought and struggled for – they had not pulled down one king just to create another! Cromwell also seemed to believe that the fall of Charles I and monarchy demonstrated that God did not like kings and had 'witnessed against them'. Ultimately, Cromwell could not square his conscience and his understanding of God's will with acceptance of the crown.

90. THE HUMBLE PETITION AND ADVICE MADE CROMWELL 'KING IN ALL BUT NAME'

Despite his refusal of the crown, the Humble Petition and Advice, adopted on 25 May 1657, made significant changes to the position of the Lord Protector. He could now name his own successor and provision was made for an 'other house' apart from the House of Commons, appointments to which were to be made by Cromwell. The Humble Petition thus created a hereditary position of Lord Protector vested in the Cromwell family and the possibility of creating a Cromwellian aristocracy through the 'other house'. Cromwell was installed for a second time as Lord Protector on 26 June after a magnificent procession through the streets of London to Westminster Hall. There an elaborate ceremony of investiture was performed; Cromwell was robed in purple, presented with a sword and a Bible and seated on the coronation chair that had been brought from Westminster Abbey. Cromwell may have refused the crown but in many other respects the protectoral regime was increasingly taking on the prerogatives and trappings of monarchy.

91. 'Old Nick' Came For 'Old Noll'

On Friday 3 September 1658, a violent storm raged over London – trees were uprooted and roofs damaged. In Whitehall Palace Cromwell lay dying. The slow and painful death from cancer of his beloved daughter, Elizabeth, a month before seems to have broken his spirit and thereafter he declined rapidly. Cromwell's doctors believed he was suffering from 'a double tertian ague', what we would now call a form of malaria.* Contemporaries were all too aware of the significance of the date: on 3 September 1650 Cromwell had defeated the Scots at the Battle of Dunbar, exactly a year later he had beaten Charles II and his Scots-Royalist army at the Battle of Worcester. It was said that before Worcester, Cromwell had sold his soul to the Devil in return for seven years of power. As the storm raged over Whitehall, Cromwell died on the afternoon of the 3rd; many shook their heads and said, 'Old Nick's come for Old Noll.'

*Fitzgibbons, J., *Cromwell's Head* (Kew: The National Archives), 2008, p. 8.

92. Richard Cromwell Was Nick-Named 'Tumble-Down Dick'

When the exiled Royalists heard of Cromwell's death in September 1658 they rejoiced, believing that without him the Protectorate must fall. But his son and designated successor, Richard Cromwell (1626–1712), was proclaimed Lord Protector in his father's place and the ceremony of installation took place in Westminster Hall. There was no revolt in the army and no Royalist risings in the country. The Protectorate seemed to have achieved stability and the Royalist exiles were very downhearted. But Richard was a very different man from his father. He had never served in the army and had no military experience. He had no particularly strong religious convictions and had spent most of his adult life as a country gentleman managing his estates. As such he did not understand the mentality of either the army or the Independent congregations that had supported Oliver. He did not seem to appreciate the power the army had over the Protectorate and he tended to favour the civilian members of the government over the Army Grandees.

Richard's government not only faced rising tensions between civilian and military members, it was also bankrupt. The war with Spain, begun at the end of 1654, was ruinously expensive. Maintaining the fleet and the army on a permanent war footing was very costly and despite the continuing high levels of taxation it was not enough to stop the government falling ever further into debt. The high taxes were also undermining what little sympathy there was for the Protectorate in the country.

Faced with bankruptcy, Richard began to think about ways of ending the Spanish war and reducing the military budget. This alarmed the Grandees who feared that their power and influence would be reduced if they were brought under civilian control and the size of the army reduced. Richard was also opposed by the same coalition of republicans and Commonwealth men who had always opposed the Protectorate. Also, 1659 witnessed a revival of Leveller activity and radicalism in the army caused by a sense among junior officers and the rank-and-file that the 'good old cause' had been betrayed.

In April, Richard attempted to dissolve the Council of Officers but this was blocked by the officers in league with the republicans. At the same time, petitions came in from the army and the country calling for the restoration of the Commonwealth. Finally, at the end of May, his government paralysed by opposition, Richard accepted the inevitable and resigned. The Protectorate was dissolved along with the upper house, and the army invited the surviving MPs ejected in April 1653 to return to Westminster and reconstitute the Commonwealth.

Richard retired to his estate at Hursley, Hampshire, which he had acquired in 1643, but at the Restoration he thought it safer both to elude the returning Stuarts and his numerous creditors and in July 1660 he sailed for the Continent. He toured Spain and Italy, but lived mainly in Paris. In 1680 or 1681 Richard returned to England, living at Finchley, Middlesex, and later at Cheshunt, Hertfordshire. He died in 1712 and was buried in Hursley parish church, where a modern memorial records his presence.

93. After the Fall of Richard Cromwell the Army Took Control

The restored Rump elected a Council of State as an executive body and a Committee of Seven to oversee the army. Known Cromwellians and servants of the Protectorate were purged from both the army and the civil administration. But the same problem remained: was the army the servant of the state or its master? Would it obey orders it did not like issued by a civilian government? This dilemma was highlighted again in August 1659 when a Royalist rising occurred in Cheshire led by Sir George Booth. John Lambert took a detachment of the New Model north and easily crushed Booth's rebellion. It demonstrated yet again that the Rump owed its existence entirely to the support and protection of the army.

Unfortunately, the MPs in Westminster were reluctant to accept this fact. They still believed that the army would obey their orders. In September, officers from Lambert's regiment petitioned Parliament for reform of the government. The outraged MPs reprimanded the impertinence of the officers, and forbade any further petitioning by the army. Some MPs even called for the arrest of Lambert. On 12 October, Parliament provoked Lambert still further by revoking his commission, along with those of eight other senior officers. Lambert's response was to march on Westminster the next day and forcibly dissolve the Rump. But what was going to happen now and who was to carry on the business of government?

Lambert and his junta set up a Committee of Safety to consider how the government might be reconstituted. Many thought that Lambert or Captain-General Fleetwood might set themselves up as a new Lord Protector. Some regiments had remained loyal to the Rump and had tried to resist Lambert's coup of the 13th. There had almost been a pitched battle in Whitehall between pro- and anti-Lambert units. It was an ominous sign that the unity of the army was beginning to break apart. Another straw in the wind was the declaration General Monck sent from Scotland condemning the coup and demanding the restoration of the Rump; meanwhile the country began to stir.

On 3 December, the town of Portsmouth denounced the coup and declared its support for the Rump. Fighting and riots broke out in London between soldiers and civilians with the people calling for a 'free Parliament' and the end of military rule. On the 13th both the fleet and the army in Ireland declared for the Rump. Lambert, Fleetwood and the military junta were losing control of the situation. By Christmas 1659, people were wondering who was actually running the country, there was a tax strike and local officials refused to discharge their duties until a more legitimate government was restored. On 26 December, Lambert and the junta gave up the struggle and restored the Rump; a faction of the army had clutched directly at power and failed. Meanwhile, on 8 December General Monck established his headquarters on the Scots-English border at Coldstream; on 1 January 1660 he began to march south.

94. GENERAL MONCK AND HIS ARMY MARCHED INTO ENGLAND IN JANUARY 1660

George Monck began the Civil War as a Royalist and was captured in January 1644. With the defeat of the King in 1646 Monck took an oath of loyalty to Parliament, was released and served in Ireland where he secured Ulster for Parliament during the second Civil War in 1648. During the Scottish campaign Monck quickly gained the friendship and confidence of Cromwell, who, as we have seen, appointed him to command the English forces in Scotland. From 1652 to 1654 Monck served as a General-at-Sea successfully fighting the Dutch. Cromwell sent him back to Scotland in 1654 where he remained for the next five years. A firm supporter of Cromwell and the Protectorate, Monck slowly remodelled his army in Scotland, purging Levellers, Quakers, Fifth Monarchists and similar radicals and replacing them with conservative officers of moderate religious and political views. Monck successfully created a disciplined and cohesive army that shared his own political and religious outlook. When Cromwell died, Monck immediately pledged his loyalty to Richard and regretted the fall of the Protectorate. Following events in England through 1659 Monck became even more convinced that the army leaders were behaving irresponsibly in opposing civilian rule and, as we have seen, condemned the military coup of 13 October.

When Monck marched out of Coldstream on 1 January 1660 he had been very careful not to reveal his political intentions. In Yorkshire he met with Sir Thomas Fairfax who had been in retirement since 1650 and it is possible that they discussed the feasibility of a restoration of the monarchy. Meanwhile, the restored Rump was busy purging the army of those who had supported the coup. Monck finally arrived in London on 3 February, but had still not declared his intentions. Would he support the Rump? Would he make himself Lord Protector? Would he restore the king?

Unrest in the country centred around the demand for a 'free Parliament'; that is, a full Parliament, elected using the old franchise, with no exclusion of those not 'well-affected'. Everyone knew that if the country was allowed to express its choice there would be an overwhelming demand for the restoration of the monarchy. The first step in such a process was the dissolution of the Rump and this was achieved on 11 February when Monck demanded that the Rump readmit those surviving MPs who had been expelled by Colonel Pride back in December 1648. The Rump had no alternative but to comply and when the news broke that the Long Parliament was to reconvene, London went wild with joy.

95. The Declaration of Breda Prepared the Way for the Restoration of Charles II

Parliament, including the excluded members, met on 21 February 1660 and on 16 March voted its own dissolution and called for a free general election. The Long Parliament, which had first met in November 1640, had finally come to an end. Meanwhile, Lambert was imprisoned in the Tower, he escaped on 10 April and tried to rally opposition to the changes happening in London and to the prospect of a restoration, but his small force was overwhelmed at Daventry soon afterwards and he returned as a prisoner to London. When the elections had been held and the new Parliament – the Convention Parliament – met on 25 April only sixteen former Rump MPs had been re-elected. The new Parliament was overwhelmingly Royalist and conservative Presbyterian in character.

At the beginning of April, Charles II had, from exile in Holland, issued the Declaration of Breda, a very significant document in which the King reassured opinion in England that a restored monarchy would work through Parliament and that there would not be extensive reprisals levelled against those who had fought his father or served the Commonwealth and Protectorate. The Declaration reassured many that it was safe to restore the Stuart. At the beginning of May 1660 the Convention declared that the only legitimate government in England was one vested in King, Lords and Commons and they formally invited Charles II to return. On 8 May they declared that Charles had been king since the moment of his father's execution on 30 January 1649. In other words, the intervening eleven years had simply not happened and all the acts and ordinances of the Commonwealth and Protectorate were invalid. On 25 May Charles landed at Dover amid scenes of great rejoicing and celebration. The ship in which he sailed from Holland to England had left harbour called the *Naseby*, en route to Holland it was rechristened the *Royal Charles*. From Dover, Charles made a triumphal progress towards London, finally entering the capital on 29 May, his thirtieth birthday, amid scenes of wild rejoicing.

96. Some of the Surviving Regicides Were Hung, Drawn and Quartered

Charles II was intelligent enough to know that it would be a mistake to unleash a Royalist terror on his return. On the contrary, his priority was to try and put aside the enmities and divisions of the previous twenty years and, on 29 August, the Convention Parliament passed an Act of Indemnity and Oblivion pardoning the vast majority of those who had fought for Parliament or served the Commonwealth and Protectorate. However, some scores had to be settled and the Act of Indemnity and Oblivion excluded those who had either signed Charles I's death warrant or had played a significant role in his trial and execution.

Many regicides had died before the Restoration, such as Cromwell, John Bradshaw and Henry Ireton, but the survivors who were in custody were brought to trial in October 1660 and ten were condemned to death for treason. Six of the condemned had signed the death warrant. Francis Hacker and Daniel Axtell had commanded the guard during Charles I's trial and execution, Hugh Peter had preached enthusiastically to anyone who would listen on the justice of the sentence passed on the King and John Cook was the King's prosecutor at the trial. A further nineteen regicides were sentenced to life imprisonment.

On 30 January 1661, the first anniversary of the execution of Charles I after the Restoration, the bodies of Cromwell, Ireton and Bradshaw were dug up and their decaying remains were hung in gibbets at Tyburn. Their remains were then buried in a pit under the gallows and their heads displayed on spikes outside Westminster Hall. Twenty regicides managed to escape abroad, either to Switzerland, Holland or America. One of them, John Lisle, was murdered by a Royalist agent in Lausanne in 1664. In 1663, three regicides who had fled to Holland, John Barkstead, John Okey and Miles Corbet, were extradited, tried and executed.

The thirteen executed all faced their ordeal with great courage and some took the opportunity provided by their trial and public execution to restate their conviction that what they had done was just, necessary and the work of God. Moreover, they were proud that what they had done had been done openly and in 'the clear light of day'. They also faced their grisly executions – hanging, drawing and quartering – with great courage and fortitude. Charles II was wise to keep the killings and the revenge to a minimum. The theatre of the trials and executions provided a platform from where the condemned could justify their conduct and face their deaths as heroes and martyrs.

97. Cromwell's Head Was Stuck on a Spike at Westminster Hall

As we have just seen, on the morning of 30 January 1661 the bodies of Cromwell, Ireton and Bradshaw were taken from their tombs in Westminster Abbey to Tyburn, where they were all hanged from gallows. Later that day the bodies were cut down and the heads were cut off. The headless carcases were thrown into a pit adjacent to the gallows (which means that the headless remains of Cromwell lie somewhere under the thundering traffic of Hyde Park Corner.) The heads were then stuck on top of metal-tipped poles and placed over the main entrance to Westminster Hall.

There Cromwell's head remained until the late 1680s when, the story goes, it was blown down in a gale and retrieved by a sentinel who, realising what it was, took it home and hid it. The head then passed through various owners until in 1815 it was bought by one Josiah Wilkinson. It remained in the Wilkinson family until 1960 when Horace Wilkinson bequeathed the head to Cromwell's old College, Sidney Sussex, Cambridge. The head, complete with the remains of the metal spike, was buried discretely in the antechapel of the college and a plaque erected to commemorate the fact.

98. The Restoration of the Ancien Régime Was Almost Spontaneous

Throughout the summer of 1660 the old order in church and state gradually reasserted itself. Parliament declared that most of the acts and ordinances of the last twenty years were void, the Triennial Act and the act making it illegal for the king to dissolve Parliament without its consent were repealed. Oaths of loyalty to the King were imposed on all office holders. The New Model Army was paid off and disbanded. The land question was also settled far more easily than most people expected. The lands of the Crown and the Church had been confiscated and passed to new owners, but this land was largely recovered, the new owners compensated, and it was returned to the Crown and the Church. In the few years following the restoration, most Royalists who had lost their estates during the wars managed to recover their lands so that ultimately there was not a significant change in the pattern of landownership and Charles II enjoyed most of the privileges and prerogatives of his father. What were not restored were the prerogative courts of High Commission, Star Chamber and the councils of Wales and the North. Neither was the legislation outlawing Ship Money and other prerogative taxes repealed.

The question of religion loomed large in 1660. Most believed that a national Church of England should be re-established, but that it should be one which was broad enough and flexible enough in its doctrine and liturgy to include not only Anglicans but also the vast majority of English Presbyterians; the term used for such a broad Church was 'comprehension'. A series of meetings were held between leading Presbyterians and Anglicans to try and hammer out the details of this comprehensive Church settlement. However, in May 1661 a new Parliament assembled; the Cavalier Parliament, as it came to be called, was much more aggressively Anglican and Royalist than its predecessor and far less interested in comprehension. Also, in many ways, the old Church of England was restoring itself without any help from Parliament. Bishops and deans returned to their cathedrals, ejected clergy returned to their parishes. Churchwardens and parishioners set up the royal arms again in their churches and brought out of hiding copies of the *Book of Common Prayer* and carried on where they had been obliged to leave off in the mid-1640s.

During the summer of 1661 Convocation, the governing body of the Church of England, revised the Prayer Book and in May 1662 Parliament passed an Act of Uniformity, which turned its back on any idea of comprehension and re-established an Episcopal Church. The act declared that everyone in England must be a member of the Church of England and must use the liturgy contained in the revised *Book of Common Prayer*. Any expression of organised religion outside the Church of England was forbidden. It also declared that all officiating clergy must have been ordained by a bishop, a provision that hit many Presbyterian ministers very hard. The clergy were required to swear an oath to uphold the monarchy, the establishment and to abide by every requirement and rubric of the new Prayer Book. They were given until St Bartholomew's Day – 24 August – to take the oath or resign their posts. In the end, over 2,000 clergymen refused to take the oath and left the church. One achievement of the Act of Uniformity was to make religious dissent a permanent feature of the English religious landscape for the next 300 years.

99. In Scotland the 'English Civil War' Is Called 'The War in the Three Kingdoms'

It seems odd that a war that began in Scotland in 1638–39, which included Ireland and Wales and ended with the defeat of a largely Scottish army at Worcester in 1651, should be called the 'English' Civil War. It is time to stand back from the narrative of events and consider how the civil wars have been understood and interpreted since 1660. First of all, let us consider how historians have written about the wars – what is called 'historiography'. Almost from the moment the fighting ended people were writing about what had happened. One of the most influential histories was that written by Edward Hyde, Lord Clarendon. Hyde had been a member of Charles I's council during the civil wars and had served Charles II when he was Prince of Wales and later as King. Between 1660 and 1667 Hyde was Lord Chancellor. He was in a unique position to write about the wars as he had known most of the principal players and been involved in many of the events and issues we have discussed. His great *History of the Rebellion and Civil Wars in England* was published between 1702 and 1704.

For all Hyde's first-hand knowledge, he was a Royalist, and at the end of the seventeenth century and through the eighteenth century a lively debate was carried on by Whig and Tory historians over the Civil War and the wars became one more battlefield in party polemics. In the nineteenth century the historiography of the Civil War was dominated by Lord Macauley, whose monumental history of England immortalised the 'Whig interpretation of history'. This stated that history should be read in terms of the eventual victory of Parliamentary democracy and progress over absolute monarchy. In this reading the civil wars become an important staging post on the inevitable victory of Parliament over the Crown.

Towards the end of the nineteenth century a more detached and 'scientific' approach to history developed as historians became more professional and based their work upon close reading of contemporary archives. Historians such as Samuel Gardiner and R. H. Tawney moved away from the party polemic of earlier histories and criticised the Whig interpretation. They emphasised the economic factors involved in the causes of the Civil War and the religious question. The twentieth century witnessed a great development of academic history and research on the subject of the Civil War. Issues such as the 'gentry debate', the county community, religious and political radicalism etc. have transformed our understanding of the Civil War and its social, economic and religious causes.

It is also a feature of the Civil War that there has never been any consensus about what to call it!

Here are some of the titles that have been applied to the wars:

The Great Rebellion
The English Civil War
The Puritan Revolution
The English Revolution
The Wars of the Three Kingdoms
The British Civil Wars
Was it one civil war, or a series of smaller, discrete civil wars – was it a singular or a plural experience...?

100. The Significance of the Civil War Is Still Being Debated

We have seen how the historiography of the Civil War has changed over the centuries and in the same vein the significance of the events of 1640–60 have been fiercely contested. In the immediate aftermath of the Restoration everything was done to pretend that the events of 1640—60 simply had not happened. Charles II's reign was deemed to have started on 30 January 1649, not 29 May 1660, the Church of England was re-established much as it had been in the 1630s, the law courts carried on in the same old ways. The ideas of the Levellers and Diggers were, apparently, forgotten and the old hierarchies in society and between men and women, masters and servants, lords and commons were reaffirmed.

In the seventeenth century the term 'revolution' meant just that: a revolving through 360 degrees so that you ended up back where you started. In that sense, the events of 1640–60 are a classic example of a revolution. But that is not how we understand the word today and using the modern understanding of the term the question is much more problematic. Perhaps this is because, with very few exceptions, the men who made the 'revolution' were not revolutionaries.

Yet anyone who walked by Westminster Hall after the Restoration would have seen the rotting skulls of Cromwell, Bradshaw and Ireton on their spikes, church sermons often included references to the wars and the regicide as warnings of what happens when 'the people' slipped the bridle of obedience and deference; and every year on 30 January and 29 May the regicide and the Restoration were solemnly commemorated across the land – with fasting and repentance for the former and joy and thanksgiving for the latter. However, much

Restoration England tried to forget the events of 1640–60 they could not easily be ignored. In the longer term a series of fundamental political and social questions and problems were left unresolved in 1660, chief among them were the relationship between the monarchy and Parliament and the place of religion, which continued to bedevil political life throughout the reign of Charles II.

In retrospect we can ask the following questions:

- Did the experience of the civil wars have any influence on the rise of Whig and Tory parties in the 1680s?
- Did the memory of the civil wars influence the decision of the Church of England and the political nation to oppose the rule of the Catholic James II and invite William of Orange to take his place in the so-called 'Glorious Revolution' of 1688?
- Did the experience of the wars and the radical ideas it generated play any part in the American and French Revolutions of the next century?
- Did the wars have any influence on the development of Parliamentary democracy and constitutional monarchy in Great Britain?
- Why were the writings of the Levellers and Diggers largely forgotten until unearthed by historians in the late nineteenth century, and what became of the petition of the Leveller women to be considered equal with men and given the vote?
- What effect did the defeat of Puritanism in 1660 have upon the English dissenting tradition?

All these questions, and more, have been debated ever since the Restoration and I hope that having finished this book you will be inspired to go on and join in that debate. And when you've considered all those aspects, here is a final thought from C. V. Wedgwood: 'The final, dispassionate, authoritative history of the Civil Wars cannot be written until the problems have ceased to matter; by that time it will not be worth writing.'*

*Wedgwood, C. V., *The King's Peace: 1637–41* (London: Collins, 1955), p. 14.

Also available from Amberley Publishing

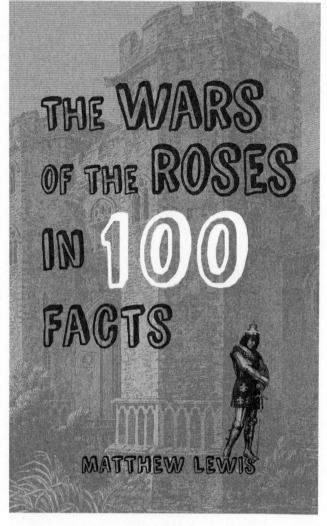

Available from all good bookshops or to order direct
978 1 4456 4746 3
Please call 01453-847-800
www.amberleybooks.com